Second Language Listening: Theory and Practice

CAMBRIDGE LANGUAGE EDUCATION
Series Editor: Jack C. Richards

Second Language Listening

Theory and Practice

John Flowerdew
City University of Hong Kong

Lindsay Miller
City University of Hong Kong

CAMBRIDGE
UNIVERSITY PRESS

CAMBRIDGE UNIVERSITY PRESS
Cambridge, New York, Melbourne, Madrid, Cape Town, Singapore, São Paulo

Cambridge University Press
40 West 20th Street, New York, NY 10011-4211, USA

www.cambridge.org
Information on this title: www.cambridge.org/9780521781350

© John Flowerdew and Lindsay Miller 2005

First published 2005

Printed in the United States of America

A catalog record for this book is available from the British Library.

Library of Congress Cataloging in Publication Data

Flowerdew, John, 1951–
Second language listening : theory and practice / John Flowerdew, Lindsay Miller.
    p.   cm. – (Cambridge language education)
Includes bibliographical references and index.
ISBN 0-521-78135-3 – ISBN 0-521-78647-9 (pbk.)
1. Language and languages – Study and teaching.   2. Listening – Study and teaching.
I. Miller, Lindsay   II. Title.   III. Series.
P53.47.F58   2005
418′.0071–dc22   2003066738

ISBN-13   978-0-521-78135-0 hardback
ISBN-10   0-521-78135-3 hardback

ISBN-13   978-0-521-78647-8 paperback
ISBN-10   0-521-78647-9 paperback

Contents

Series editor's preface

Acquiring good listening and speaking skills in English is the main concern of many second and foreign language learners, and today's English teacher needs to be well versed in current approaches to the teaching of the aural/oral skills. Second language listening, relatively ignored for many years within applied linguistics, has today come into its own. Although still somewhat neglected in second language acquisition research, listening now plays a more central role in language teaching. University entrance exams, school leaving tests, and other examinations have begun to include a listening component, an acknowledgment that listening ability is an important aspect of second language proficiency.

The nature of listening comprehension is also now better understood. Earlier views of listening saw it as the mastery of discrete skills or microskills, which formed the focus of teaching and testing. A skills approach focused on such things as discriminating sounds in words (especially phonemic contrasts), deducing the meaning of unfamiliar words, predicting content, differentiating between fact and opinion, and noting contradictions, inadequate information, and ambiguities.

The changed status of listening in recent years was partly prompted by Krashen's emphasis on the role of comprehension and comprehensible input in triggering language development. In the 1980s and 1990s, applied linguists also began to borrow new theoretical models of comprehension from the field of cognitive psychology. It was from this source that the distinction between bottom-up processing and top-down processing was derived – a distinction that led to an awareness of the importance of background knowledge and schema in comprehension. Listeners were viewed as actively involved in constructing meaning based on expectations, inferences, intentions, prior knowledge, and selective processing of the input. Listening came to be viewed as an interpretive process. At the same time, the fields of conversation analysis and discourse analysis were revealing a great deal about the organization of spoken discourse, leading to a realization that written texts read aloud could not provide a suitable basis for developing the abilities needed to process real-time authentic discourse. Authenticity in materials became a catchword and part of a pedagogy of teaching listening that is now well established.

Second Language Listening examines these issues and provides a valuable overview of recent and current approaches to the role of listening in language teaching. The authors present a highly readable account of the linguistic, psycholinguistic, cultural, interactional, and pragmatic factors involved in understanding spoken discourse. They also describe an original pedagogical model of second language listening that reflects the complexities of the listening process. They then show how the model can be used to evaluate published materials and to develop criteria for planning, evaluating, and creating listening materials and programs, including both conventional textbook materials and materials employing new technology. The authors include illuminating case studies from a range of contexts to show how listening can be taught and assessed at different levels.

Second Language Listening should therefore serve as a valuable resource for teachers, curriculum developers, and others concerned with the nature of second language listening processes.

Jack C. Richards

Preface

For a long time, listening has been treated as the Cinderella of the four macro-skills: speaking, listening, reading, and writing. However, as an essential part of communicative competence, listening is a skill that deserves equal treatment with the others, both in the classroom and in the preparation of language teachers. With the unrelenting trend toward globalization, which manifests itself in greater international trade, travel, education, Internet use, cheap international telephone calls, and mass entertainment, English has become a world language. The need to be able to understand English is increasing by the day. There is a growing need, therefore, for international citizens to be able to understand not just standard British or American spoken English, but other varieties spoken around the world.

Second Language Listening: Theory and Practice combines up-to-date listening theory, a pedagogical model developed by the authors, and case studies of pedagogical practice. The volume draws on the authors' own research and experience, where appropriate, but is eclectic in encompassing a full range of current views on theory and practice. Each chapter contains tasks and discussion questions that contextualize the material and encourage readers to engage with the concepts presented.

Textbooks are normally viewed as presenting established bodies of knowledge to uninitiated students. In *Second Language Listening: Theory and Practice*, we have tried to go a little beyond this traditional approach by incorporating our own innovative pedagogical model of listening. This is introduced in Chapter 6 and applied in subsequent chapters, which deal with materials and methodology, primarily by means of a range of case studies.

The book is divided into three parts. Part I is entitled "Historical Background." In Chapter 1, we look at the main approaches that have been taken to language teaching over the years and the role of listening in these approaches. The approaches are grammar-translation, direct-method, grammar-based, audio-lingual, discrete-item, communicative, task-based, learner-strategy, and integrated. After introducing each approach, we identify the main learning goal for listening and, where appropriate, exemplify and critique each approach with a textbook task. Chapter 2 describes current models of the listening process. After brief descriptions of speech recognition, listening developments in the L1, and long- and short-term memory, we describe three models: the bottom-up, the top-down, and the interactive models. Chapter 3 describes what a spoken message consists of in terms of the different types of meaning it may convey: phonological, syntactic, semantic, pragmatic, and kinesic. All these elements of meaning play a role in comprehension, although deficiencies in one area can be made up for in others. Chapter 4 describes the features of spoken language that distinguish it from written text and the differences between monologue and dialogue. Considerable attention is given to the specific features of spoken interaction, such as turn-taking, topic shift, back-channeling, and repair. Chapter 5 discusses different learning styles and strategies for listening. We describe the extensive work on general learner strategies that has been conducted over the past 25 years and then focus in particular on learner strategies in L2 listening. The chapter concludes with an example of a strategies-based approach to teaching listening.

In Part II, "A Pedagogical Model and Its Application," we present and apply our own model of second language listening. In Chapter 6, we map out what we consider to be the essential features of such a model. In addition to the psycholinguistic theories presented in Chapter 2, our model incorporates a set of dimensions that we have derived from a range of theories relevant to listening. These dimensions are eclectic insofar as they draw on cognitive, social, linguistic, and pedagogic theory. Drawn together, they can enable us to develop a unified model of second language listening. These dimensions make the model individualized, cross-cultural, social, contextualized, affective, strategic, intertextual, and critical. It is stressed that not all of these dimensions will apply at any one time, but any of them may be drawn upon, where appropriate, in the design, adaptation, or evaluation of pedagogic materials. In Chapter 7, we examine listening materials from a variety of modern textbooks. Each activity, from beginner to advanced, is evaluated in light of the model presented in Chapter 6. Chapter 8 presents a series of case studies of a range of pedagogic listening situations – a primary school course, an academic listening course, a radio series, a self-access context for listening, and an intensive English language course. Each of the case studies is again evaluated in light of the pedagogic model presented in Chapter 6.

Part III, "Key Issues in Teaching and Testing," consists of three chapters. Chapter 9 deals with the role of technology. Radio, audio recordings, the language laboratory, video, and computer-assisted listening are all considered in relation to their ability to facilitate listening pedagogy. In Chapter 10, we focus on questioning techniques and analyze the different types of questioning formats: display versus referential, closed versus open, the use of the L1 versus the L2, focus on form versus focus on function, visually supported versus nonvisually supported, and individual versus group. Chapter 11 is devoted to testing. Three approaches to the testing of listening are introduced: the discrete-point approach, the integrative approach, and the communicative approach. It is suggested that the communicative approach is best suited to the pedagogical model of listening presented in Part II.

The book includes an appendix, "Concluding Questions for Reflection," which can be used by the reader to reflect on issues examined in the book and by tutors using the text as a course book.

Second Language Listening: Theory and Practice is designed to be used by both pre- and in-service teachers. It has been extensively piloted with both preservice BA-TESL students and MA part-time in-service teachers. Although the examples used in the book are from the perspective of English as a foreign or second language, the book may also be used by students and teachers of languages other than English.

Note: Transcriptions in the book reflect the contributor's original work and have not been altered to reflect American English.

John Flowerdew
Lindsay Miller

Acknowledgments

We are grateful to the following people who have assisted us in various ways with the book: Jack Richards, for inviting us to take part in this series; Mary Sandre, Debbie Goldblatt, Angela Castro, and Julia Hough, the editorial team at CUP New York, for having the patience to work with us; Virginia Costa, for proofreading and valuable advice about earlier drafts of the manuscript; June Titheridge, for reading and commenting on the final draft; BA-TESL and MA-TESL students at the City University of Hong Kong, for allowing us to pilot the materials with them; staff and students at Cambridge University, the University of Salzburg, and Baptist University, Hong Kong, for useful feedback on seminar presentations of the model presented in Chapter 6; Gunther Kress, for comments, also on Chapter 6; Professor Gillian Brown of the University of Cambridge, who read the manuscript and gave valuable comments, as did Dr. John Williams, also of the University of Cambridge; Dino Mahoney, for the information regarding the technology case study; Jackie Newbrook and the staff at Bell School, Safron Walden, for the information about the self-access case study; Henry C. F. Li and the staff of Kai Chi Primary School, for information about the young learners case study; Randi Reppen, for the information about the intensive language course at Northern Arizona University; Richard W. Forest, for help with proofreading; and Jasper Chan Chap Choi, for assistance with the computer work. We also acknowledge the very useful feedback provided by the anonymous reviewers of the manuscript.

PART I:
HISTORICAL BACKGROUND

In Part I of this book, we present the main theoretical aspects that have traditionally been considered when discussing how learners develop listening skills. We begin in Chapter 1 by outlining the main approaches and methods that have been used over the past 70 years or so to teach English in general, and then we comment on how listening has, or has not, been accommodated in each approach and method.

In Chapter 2, we describe current psycholinguistic models of the listening process. Most approaches to teaching listening in the past have been influenced by three models – the so-called *bottom-up, top-down*, and *interactive* models. These models are still important, and we maintain that knowledge of how they operate is essential to understanding how an approach to the teaching of listening may be developed.

The main approaches to listening are influenced by our knowledge of the different types of meaning involved in understanding spoken text and how they affect the ways in which we listen to messages. These elements are reviewed in Chapter 3.

Chapter 4 takes the reader one stage deeper in the process of understanding the particular features of spoken text and how these features play a prominent role in any model that tries to account for how we listen. Attention is given to both monologue and, important for us, dialogue.

If learners are to develop skills in manipulating the features and elements of listening, they need to be aware of their specific learning styles and strategies and how these can affect the way they listen to spoken text. This is the theme of Chapter 5, the last chapter of Part I.

Each of the chapters in Part I forms an integral approach to the type of background knowledge that is important to consider if we wish to develop an integrated model of listening. This will be our task in the second part of the book.

1 Approaches to Language Teaching and the Role of Listening

1.1 Introduction

In this first chapter, we look at the main approaches that have been used to teach listening. These approaches have, to a large extent, followed the approaches to general syllabus design and teaching methodology. As these general approaches have changed over the past 50 years, so new methods for teaching listening have been advocated. Different approaches to listening can be seen by examining exercises and tasks in published material. Richards (1993:3) states that one view of how to improve teaching is through the use of instructional materials, so that "quality of teaching will come about through the use of instructional materials that are based on findings of current theory and research." Richards (ibid.) maintains that instructional materials can have a profound effect on teaching and that teachers rely on such materials to define the language courses they teach. He quotes one teacher who talked about some new materials she tried out: "This book has totally turned around the listening program in our school. We really didn't know what to do with listening before" (p. 6).

The approaches we discuss here are the grammar-translation approach, the direct-method approach, the grammar approach, the audio-lingual approach, the discrete-item approach, the communicative approach, the task-based approach, the learner-strategy approach, and the integrated approach. After introducing each approach, we identify the main learning goal with respect to listening. These learning goals are based on Morley (1995). Although some of these may not be considered bona fide approaches themselves, we consider them all to be "approaches" because they have influenced the ways in which language has been taught. Beginning in Section 1.4, we exemplify each approach to listening with an activity and then comment on the activity.

1.2 The Grammar-Translation Approach

Traditionally, listening was not taught in language classes. The first languages taught in modern classroom settings were Latin and Greek. The purpose of learning these languages was primarily to learn their grammars. The grammar-translation approach viewed language as a descriptive set of finite rules that, once learned, gave access to the language. A grammar-translation syllabus consisted of two components: grammar and lexical items. These were presented to the learner according to their perceived degree of difficulty. Richards and Rogers (2001:5–6) list the components that made up a grammar-translation syllabus. Stated briefly, these are the following:

1. The main goal of learning the language is to be able to read its literature.
2. Reading and writing are the main focus.
3. Vocabulary is taught through translation.
4. The method focuses on translating sentences into and out of the L2.
5. Accuracy is important, as all learning leads to an exam.
6. Grammar is taught deductively.
7. The L1 is the medium of instruction.

Learning goals related to listening: None.

Comment

Listening is not mentioned at all in the preceding description of the grammar-translation approach. The only listening that students would have to do would be to listen to a description of the rules of the second language (L2) in the first language (L1). As a result, if/when the L2 was used, the focus of any listening would have been on translation of lexical items or grammar structures. One reason for the lack of any real listening in the grammar-translation approach was that students were learning "dead" languages, languages that they would not have the opportunity to listen to, so the purpose in learning those languages was to be able to translate and read literature. Another reason was that the teachers of Latin and Greek had no training in how to teach listening. And in the early days of language teaching, there were no electronic means of recording.

1.3 The Direct-Method Approach

The direct-method approach to language teaching (also known as both the natural method and the conversational method) came about as a reaction to the grammar-translation approach. Whereas the grammar-translation approach was organized around a step-by-step method of learning the rules of a language, often through the use of the first language, the direct-method approach was based on the idea that learners can best learn what is "natural" to them and that an aural/oral system of teaching them was appropriate for this purpose. This aural/oral method relied for its effectiveness on the use of monolingual teaching, that is, the L2 was the only language used in the class by the teacher and students.

The tenets of the direct-method approach are summarized by Richards and Rogers (2001) as follows:

1. Classroom instruction was conducted exclusively in the target language.
2. Only everyday vocabulary and sentences were taught.
3. Oral communication skills were built up in a carefully graded progression organized around question-and-answer exchanges between teachers and students in small, intensive classes.
4. Grammar was taught inductively.
5. New teaching points were introduced orally.
6. Concrete vocabulary was taught through demonstration, objects, and pictures; abstract vocabulary was taught through association of ideas.
7. Both speech and listening comprehension were taught.
8. Correct pronunciation and grammar were emphasized.

Gottlieb Heness and Lambert Sauveur were two of the first teachers to adopt the direct-method approach in their teaching in the late nineteenth century in the United States (see Howatt 1984). Heness and Sauveur opened a language school to teach German and French using a system similar to that described earlier. Although they did not use course books, Sauveur explains a typical lesson:

Here is the finger. Look. Here is the forefinger, here is the middle finger, here is the ring-finger, here is the little finger, and here is the thumb. Do you see the finger, madame? Yes, you see the finger and I see the finger. Do you see the finger, monsieur? – Yes, I see the finger. – Do you see the forefinger, madame? – Yes, I see the forefinger. – And you monsieur? Etc.

(Sauveur 1874, as cited in Howatt 1984:200)

The direct-method approach was adopted and made popular by Maximilian Berlitz (1852–1921). Berlitz founded a chain of language schools, prepared teaching materials, and had the native-speaker instructors in the schools use a direct-method approach in teaching the students. The idea behind what was called the Berlitz method was that it was "simple, systematic, ordered, and replicable" (Howatt ibid.:206).

Learning goals related to listening: Listen and answer questions.

Comment

It appears that the direct-method approach truly focused on teaching listening skills first and other language skills later. However, in any review of early monolingual teaching methods, it seems that although the target language was used for all purposes in the classroom, there was no systematic attempt at *teaching* listening or at developing listening strategies in the learners. The teacher assumed that the students could hear what was being said and that comprehension would follow later – what Mendelson (1994) refers to as developing listening through "osmosis."

A second problem with this approach is that although it seemed to be effective at encouraging low-level language learners to make use of the target language, it was a difficult method to use above intermediate level because the complexities of the language became too challenging for the approach. For instance, as grammar always had to be learned inductively, learners wasted a lot of time trying to work out complex rules for themselves, and teachers who could speak the learners' L1 wasted time trying to convey abstract meaning using only the L2, when a simple translation would have been more efficient.

The direct method has had a significant effect on English language teaching over the past 100 years, and many of the methods that followed it contained some elements of the direct method, most notably the communicative method.

1.4 The Grammar Approach

The main idea of grammar-based listening exercises is to analyze the language by its components and reconstruct an incomplete text. By understanding the grammar of a language and the principles of how words are put together, or parsing (see Chapter 3), we can make sense of spoken text. Rost (1994:35) tells us that "[i]n order to understand utterances, we must know how words and phrases are bound to each other."

A grammar approach to listening usually has students look at a written text while they listen to a recording. This forces them to do several things: identify words by their position in the sentence, work out the relationship between words and phrases, use forward and backward inferencing cues, and make intelligent guesses based on textual cues. This approach is often favored as a classroom approach to listening. The listening exercises are treated as purely classroom-based activities, which usually have little or no relevance to the outside world, and the tasks students are asked to perform have no real-life function. They are, however, popular as testing devices and are often used for this purpose (e.g., the international TOEFL test uses this method extensively in the listening section of the test).

Learning goals related to listening: To pattern match; to test listening.

Activity 1 – An Activity Illustrating the Grammar Approach
Listen to a medical doctor talk about staying healthy. While listening, fill in the missing words in the blank spaces below.
Getting and staying fit is important for _____. It does not matter how _____ or young you are; you can, and should, do things to _____ yourself fit and healthy. Some simple ways to get fit are _____ short distances instead of using a car or bus, cutting back on snacks like _____ or chips and instead eating fruit and vegetables, and taking up more active _____ instead of watching television every day. If we start _____ a healthy lifestyle, not only will we feel better, but there will be fewer visits to the _____. Once you begin to get fit, you will want to make more changes to your _____ and become more and more healthy.

Answers:
  1. everybody   2. old   3. keep   4. walking   5. chocolate
  6. hobbies   7. adopting   8. doctors   9. lifestyle

Comment

In Activity 1, students must use words 1 to 9 to make grammatically correct sentences. In some cases, there is more than one correct answer. However, students must listen carefully to the recording to hear which missing word is used in each sentence. Such an exercise usually has no relationship to the exercises that precede or follow it. Consequently, each listening exercise is more of a *test* of listening ability than a means of developing specific listening skills. Students can read Activity 1 and make intelligent guesses about the missing words without listening to the recording at all. But the exercise requires listening for specific vocabulary. There is no attempt to teach lexical meaning or to relate the text to anything other than the task at hand. Students do not even need to understand the words to complete the blanks in Activity 1; they need only recognize the sounds. Such activities are often found in listening books specially prepared for secondary school second language learners who are examination oriented. Because of their popularity in tests, grammar-based listening tasks have a substantial wash-back effect in the language class; that is, the format of the tests influences the approach to teaching.

Task 1

Look at Activity 1 and redesign the activity to make it more meaningful. Show your redesigned activity to a partner, and explain why you now think it is more meaningful.

1.5 The Audio-Lingual Approach

The audio-lingual approach to language learning was generated by the U.S. Defense Forces language programs during and after World War II. A number of factors influenced the way foreign languages were taught after the war (e.g., the emergence of several international languages, the greater mobility of people, and the expansion of education programs; see Stern 1983 for a more detailed description). To cater to these new needs for languages, the "Army Method" was developed in the United States. This method became known as the audio-lingual approach.

The audio-lingual approach to listening emphasizes first listening to pronunciation and grammatical forms and then imitating those forms by way of drills and exercises. In describing the audio-lingual approach, Richards and Rogers (2001:58) say that "the teaching of listening comprehension, pronunciation, grammar and vocabulary are all related to development of aural fluency."

Dialogues and drills are the basis of classroom practice with this approach. Students are encouraged to listen carefully either to a taped recording of, or a teacher reading out, a dialogue or drill. They then record their own version or respond to cues from the teacher to repeat parts of the dialogue or drill. The idea behind such a technique is that it helps the learner to create good habits. It is based on the idea of contrastive analysis, in which the material writer attempts to minimize interference from the students' L1.

Lado and Fries (1954) prepared a pronunciation textbook based on this approach (see Activity 2). The audio-lingual approach became a popular teaching method in the 1960s and early 1970s, when language laboratories were in fashion. The approach can still be found, in different guises, in many current classroom textbooks.

Learning goals related to listening: To pattern match; to listen, imitate, and memorize.

Activity 2 – An Activity Illustrating the Audio-Lingual Approach

Practice the following sentences. Remember that the tongue does not contact or vibrate against the tooth ridge or palate when you pronounce [r] correctly.

What is he reading?	He's reading a book.
What is she reading?	She's reading a book.
What are they reading?	They're reading a book.
What are you reading?	I'm reading a book.
What is he writing?	He's writing some letters.
What is she writing?	She's writing some letters.
What are they writing?	They're writing some letters.
What are you writing?	I'm writing some letters.
What is he wearing?	He's wearing a green suit.
What is she wearing?	She's wearing a green suit.
What are they wearing?	They're wearing green suits.
What are you wearing?	I'm wearing a green suit.
Where is he?	He's in the garden.
Where is she?	She's in the garden.
Where are they?	They're in the garden.

English Pronunciation, by R. Lado and C. C. Fries, 1958. Reproduced by permission of The University of Michigan Press, Ann Arbor.

Comment

The approach to teaching exemplified in Activity 2 is based on the stimulus-response theory of the American school of behaviorist psychology (see Skinner 1957). Basically, the more the students repeat a "correct" phrase/sentence, the stronger their memory of the structure will be. Therefore, students must listen and repeat similar words and sentence structures many times in order to remember them. If a student makes an incorrect response, the teacher corrects the student before continuing with the exercise. The drill pattern in Activity 2 could be extended into a two-phase conversation between students:

S1: What's he reading?
S2: He's reading a book.

But it is difficult to see the dialogue extending beyond this two-phase pattern. Because there is no attempt to teach lexis or contextualize the sentences, developing listening skills is not the main focus of the audio-lingual approach; the manipulation of structures is.

Task 2
Design for elementary students a listening worksheet that uses an audio-lingual approach to teach the simple past tense.

1.6 The Discrete-Item Approach

The audio-lingual approach led to what may be called the discrete-item approach in teaching. Whereas the audio-lingual approach focuses on drilling with the intent of "understanding" grammar, a discrete-item approach deals with the *segmental* and *suprasegmental* aspects of spoken text and their contextualization. Segmentals are the individual vowel and consonant sounds. Suprasegmentals are, for example, stress and tone. A discrete-item-based approach deals with these features of speech in a highly structured way. Often sounds and features of spoken text are presented and drilled. They are then compared and contrasted with other sounds in the language as a way of trying to familiarize students with the sounds. Ur (1994) points out that many students have difficulty hearing sounds in English because these sounds may not exist in their own language (see Chapter 3). Therefore, it is "essential for the learner to achieve familiarity with the common phonemes of the target language as soon as possible if he is to be an efficient listener" (Ur 1994:12). This might suggest that a discrete-item approach should be used only at the beginning of a course and then forgotten about. Experience shows, however, that these discrimination problems persist right up to advanced levels.

It is possible, by understanding the students' first languages, to make predictions about what features of the target language they will have difficulty hearing or discriminating. For example, Japanese students have difficulty distinguishing between /v/ and /w/ and between /ɪ/ and /iː/, French students have difficulty with /e/ and /eɪ/ and with /θ/ and /ð/, and many nonnative English students have difficulty identifying -*ed* past tense endings. By knowing what sounds students will have the most difficulty with, teachers are able to customize the type of listening exercises to which their students are exposed. The types of exercises that help students practice listening to the sounds of the language are isolation-type listening tasks. That is, processing is done on a discrete-item basis. This type of listening enables students to listen for helpful cues in the text.

Learning goals related to listening: To process discrete-point information.

Activity 3 – An Activity Illustrating the Discrete-Item Approach
*There are different ways to pronounce -*ed *endings of regular past tense verbs. Listen to the following words and put them in the correct column.*

| **asked** | **followed** | **started** | **jumped** | **accepted** |
| **finished** | **lived** | **looked** | **called** | **invited** |

/t/	/d/	/ɪd/
. . . .	. . . .	. . . .
. . . .	. . . .	. . . .
. . . .	. . . .	. . . .

Comment

In Activity 3 students focus on the difference in past tense endings. This kind of activity can be found in a popular course for students called *Headway* (Cunningham and Bowler 1990), where it is usually part of larger work units on segmentals. While listening to a recording of the list of words, students arrange the words in boxes according to the sound /t/, /d/, or /ɪd/. After they have done this, they can check their answers with a key at the back of the book. Before trying this exercise, students are introduced to the different sound endings. After the exercise, they are required to mimic the sound by repeating the list of words after a taped model. The sounds are then put into sentences in the exercise that follows so that students can listen for the sound discrimination in a less isolated fashion; in subsequent exercises throughout the unit, students are exposed to these -*ed* endings in connected speech and in exercises about intonation and stress. Activity 3 would be read fairly slowly to allow students time to think about the differences and to write down the answers. However, if this were the only exercise required of students, they would be exposed to an unreal context for hearing the sounds, a common fault of the "minimal pair" type of exercises using an audio-lingual approach. In *Headway* (Cunningham and Bolwer 1990), the authors use activities such as those seen in Activity 3, but they also make an effort to contextualize the individual sounds. Most units start with a discrete-item approach to listening but then go on to encourage students to use more holistic listening strategies in later exercises.

1.7 The Communicative Approach

The communicative approach is based on the premise that what we do in the classroom should have some real-life communicative value. Real-life listening is integrated into such an approach. Littlewood (1981) states that communicative ability is nothing new to language teaching because it is also the goal of other approaches, such as situational or audio-lingual approaches. The communicative approach brings the "implications" of communication to language teaching. These implications have to do with a wider perspective on language and on language learning. The communicative approach looks at what people do with language and how they respond to what they hear.

Morrow (1981) outlines the principles on which communicative activities can be based. Stated briefly, these principles require that an activity be, in some way, communicatively useful for students; that it operate above the sentence level; that there be real-life aspects to the communication (e.g., information gaps, choice of what to say, and feedback to what has been said); that the activity involve actions (e.g., filling in a form, answering a telephone); and that mistakes be tolerated as long as they do not interfere with the communication.

Another characteristic of the communicative approach is that a variety of language, in terms of input and output, is encouraged. Students use whatever language they have to complete an activity; they should not solely use what has been taught or practiced in a particular lesson. And once the activity has started, there is little or no teacher intervention.

Learning goals related to listening: To process spoken discourse for functional purposes; to listen and interact with the speaker and/or complete a task.

Activity 4 – An Activity Illustrating the Communicative Approach
Read this situation:
You and some friends want to go out for dinner together. Listen to each other give restaurant reviews and make some notes about each restaurant. Then discuss with your friends which restaurant you think you would all like to go to. Listen for information like price, location, and quality of food and service.

Comment

Activity 4 requires students to simulate a situation in which people of their age and background might find themselves: talking with friends about going to a restaurant. The activity fulfills many of the tenets of the communicative approach: students need to perform a relevant dialogue that will allow them to use a variety of language and language skills (i.e., listening and speaking). They do not know what each person will say about the restaurants, so there is an information gap; therefore, they must listen carefully to what their friends say. There is also a choice of what to say and how to respond to what has been said; therefore, appropriate feedback to the message must be given. Such activities can be found in textbooks such as *Blueprint* (Abbs and Freebairn 1993).

Task 3
Prepare a communicative activity for an elementary group of learners based on the topic of shopping. Remember to structure the activity so that the learners will need to use a variety of listening skills for communicative purposes.

1.8 The Task-Based Approach

The main idea behind a task-based approach to developing listening is that students become *active* listeners (Brown 1987). With this approach, students are asked to listen to what are described as "authentic" situations and to "do something" with the information. This may be completing a diagram or chart, filling in a table, or drawing a picture, for example. The information is usually transferred from spoken text to a graphic form. Because the texts are authentic (usually semi-scripted), students cope with language being spoken at normal speed and with features such as accents, hesitations, fillers, and ellipses.

The result of a task-based activity can be open-ended. For example, while listening to a short lecture, students may be required to make notes and draw a simple diagram. Different students will have their own way of recording the information. The way they do this is not as important as being able to report the information they have understood. As Kumaravadivelu (1991:100) states, "In the context of task-based pedagogy the learning outcome is the result of a fairly unpredictable interaction between the task, and the task situation." Therefore, the process students employ in finding a successful outcome to the task is more important than being able to understand all the spoken text presented to them. According to the task-based approach, students need to use holistic inferential strategies.

Learning goals related to listening: To process listening for functional purposes; to listen and carry out real tasks using the information.

Activity 5 – An Activity Illustrating the Task-Based Approach
Learning how to use a public telephone
Students are given a line drawing of a public telephone. They then listen to a recorded conversation and label the drawing to show the steps in using the phone.
Extract of the tapescript

June: Okay. This is a public telephone. We have two kinds of telephones: the blue one is for international calls, while the red one is for local calls.
Carlos: I see.
June: Erm . . . do you often use public phones in Mexico?
Carlos: Yes, but I think they are a bit different from here.

June: Okay. Now, what you need to do is first get some coins, and, erm, lift the receiver and wait till you hear the dial tone. Then you put the coin in the slot and wait till you hear a different tone. Okay. Now once you hear the change in tone you can dial your number.

Carlos: Ah, yes. And do I need a local code?

June: Eh, no. Not if you are calling within the city. But if you want to call outside the city, then you need to use the other city code first. See, here next to the phone there is a list of codes.

Carlos: Okay. That is useful.

June: After you dial the number then wait till someone speaks and then press this button. Then you can speak.

Comment

There are two main points to make about task-based listening materials: (1) The tasks required of the students are usually real-life tasks that they might carry out in their L1, and (2) the texts, although presented as authentic, are usually scripted or semi-scripted. In Activity 5, the situation is realistic, telling someone how a public telephone works. The activity, though, may appear contrived. Some of us may write down instructions so that we will not forget them, but usually not. However, the student and teacher should have some way of checking that comprehension has been achieved. In large classes, the performance of a task similar to that above demonstrates success. The listening activity is for practice. As Lee (1995:325) points out, "Textually authentic materials are not inherently learner authentic." Therefore, if a recording of someone showing another person how to operate a public telephone in the street were presented, there might be background noise of people talking and traffic noises from outside, which would make the listening task very difficult when presented on an audiotape. Listening task activities can be found in textbooks such as Blundell and Stokes (1981).

Task 4

Design an authentic listening task in which the listener needs to listen and make notes. Follow the format shown in Activity 5. Design the task and illustrate the tapescript.

1.9 The Learner-Strategy Approach

A strategy-based approach to teaching listening takes as its focus the concept of learner independence. Independent learning is a stage in the process of becoming an autonomous learner, and an autonomous learner "initiates the planning and implementation of [his or her] own learning program" (Gardner and Miller 1996:vii). With this approach, the focus is on learners making decisions based on their own preferences concerning a learning task, rather than on the teacher making the decisions for them. A strategy-based approach cannot be entirely based on learner autonomy, because all learners would be free to do as they pleased and so there would be no "approach." However, as Mendelsohn (1994:116) states, "All too often, the fact that we listen to different things in different ways is overlooked in listening courses for second-language speakers." The strategy-based approach places the emphasis on learners finding out which listening strategies are effective for them and in which situations.

Some of the characteristics suggested by Mendelsohn (1994) of strategy-based activities are that they should activate the learner's schemata (i.e., how they mentally organize text or discourse); be authentic (if possible) and require learners to respond as they might in the real world; provide a large variety of exercises so that the learners have the opportunity to explore using their listening strategies in different contexts and for a variety of reasons; and enable learners to interact with the task and not simply listen and respond (i.e., learners should play an active part in, say, a dialogue, and not simply listen to it).

Based on the work of Wenden (1991) and Flavell (1979), Goh (1997) found that the Chinese students she investigated were aware of person knowledge (i.e., knowledge about themselves as learners), task knowledge (i.e., knowledge about the task they are trying to do), and strategic knowledge (i.e., knowledge about which strategies are useful to perform the task) when writing about their listening. Goh maintains that one way to help students learn about their listening is to ask them what they are already aware of and then have them share this knowledge with other students. In this way, she reasons, we help students become more autonomous and have more control over their listening skills development.

Learning goals related to listening: To develop an awareness of skills related to listening; to use a variety of listening skills effectively in achieving an objective.

Activity 6 – An Activity Illustrating the Learner-Strategy Approach

Sometimes we need to use specific listening strategies to help us understand the message. This is called having a reason for listening.

Can you think of some situations where you need to listen carefully to the message so that you can collect accurate information?

Activity: Listening for specific information

For each of the following situations, listen carefully to the cassette and write down the important information.

a. You are inviting some friends for a BBQ meal tonight, but you are not sure if the weather will be good enough to eat outside. Listen to the weather forecast and decide if you can go ahead with your plans.

b. You want to go shopping. The shops are quite far away, but you can walk there. Listen to the weather forecast and decide if you should take the bus or walk.

How did you manage to get the information you needed? Talk with your group about how you listened for the details. Did you use any special strategies?

Comment

Activity 6 illustrates a strategy-based approach to listening. Students first think and talk about how they might approach the listening task and are then given a task that is in some ways authentic. The objective of the listening activity presented here is to practice listening for specific information about the weather. However, before beginning the task, students are asked to discuss when these listening skills might be used. In this way, the students' schemata for using the skills are activated. In addition, students who may not have practiced these skills are given reasons (by their fellow students) why the skills might be useful. Students are also asked, as a prelistening task, to think of situations where they need to understand specific information. In this way, they are made aware that trying to listen for details is a useful strategy in helping them complete the task. The students are then presented with the listening task. At the end of the task the students are required to talk with each other again to find out which listening strategies they used and which were effective. More examples of developing such listening strategies can be found in Ellis and Sinclair (1989) – *Learning to Learn English*.

Task 5
Prepare for an intermediate group of students a list of "hints for listening" in different situations, similar to those in Activity 6.

1.10 The Integrated Approach

Teachers nowadays rarely use only one approach to teaching listening because our knowledge about listening as a skill has developed significantly. Additionally, textbooks now offer a variety of exercises to develop the listening skill. Not only do these exercises focus on the more traditional features of listening (e.g., listening for gist and listening for details), but they also help the students develop critical listening skills (e.g., after listening to a discussion about women's rights, the students have to present their opinions).

Many textbooks on the market deal specifically with listening. Rixon's (1987) *Listening: Upper-intermediate* is a textbook specially prepared for developing comprehension in class. In this book, an integrated approach to developing listening skills is adopted. Each unit is based on a series of prelistening, listening, and follow-up activities. Activity 7 is based on this type of format.

Learning goals related to listening: To develop listening as part of interactive communication; to develop critical listening, critical thinking, and effective speaking.

Activity 7 – A Series of Activities Illustrating the Integrated Approach
1. Prelistening: Look at a picture and tick boxes to show how you feel about a topic; predict some things you will hear about the topic; have a small debate on the topic; read a text about the topic.
2. Listening: Listen for the main ideas (complete a chart); listen for detail (fill in missing words); listen for pronunciation.
3. Follow-up: Express personal opinions; listen and complete detailed notes of exact words; look at the transcript and listen and read.

Comment

All the activities in the prelistening stage in Activity 7 activate the listeners' prior knowledge about the topic and prepare them for listening. In most of the main listening activities, students are asked to check their answers with a partner, ensuring that the lesson becomes less teacher-centered and in the hope that students will help each other by exchanging listening strategies. Many of the follow-up exercises direct the students back to the recording and ask them to consolidate their comprehension of the text. In this way, students need not feel that they will hear the text only once and need to remember everything.

Textbook writers using this approach to listening integrate listening, which is the main focus of the lesson, with reading, speaking, and writing activities. The approach is also integrated in that a variety of listening approaches are used: a discrete-item-based approach when listening for the sounds of words; a grammar-based approach when completing cloze sentences or paragraphs; a task-based approach when all the exercises build on one another around a similar topic; and a strategy-based approach when asking students to think about how they listen and to generate hints on how to listen.

1.11 Conclusion

In this chapter, we outlined and provided examples of some of the main approaches that have been adopted in dealing with listening in classroom settings. Of course, as with all teaching and learning situations, a lot of learning goes on outside the classroom. Learners may work on listening with activities very similar to those used in class. On the other hand, out-of-class listening provides the opportunity for *extensive listening* – listening for general pleasure or interest, usually to longer stretches of discourse (e.g., radio and television programs or movies). This aspect of listening should not be neglected and can be encouraged by the teacher because it promotes listening *fluency* and can be very motivating.

To summarize this chapter, language teaching methods initially did not recognize the need to teach listening, but subsequent approaches used a variety of techniques to develop specific or general listening skills. Field maintains that changes to the teaching of listening have occurred as a result of three main developments: "First, there has been a shift in perspectives, so that listening as a skill takes priority over details of language content. Secondly, there has been a wish to relate the nature of listening practised in the classroom to the kind of listening that takes place in real life. . . . Thirdly, we have become aware of the importance of providing motivation and a focus for listening" (1998: 110–11). Field goes on to propose that language teachers now must focus not only on the product of listening but also on the process. To this end, he maintains that a new methodology for teaching listening needs to be designed. Later, in Chapter 6, we propose a new model upon which such a methodology might be based.

1.12 Discussion

1. Among the approaches to listening outlined in this chapter, which approach do you mostly support? Why?
2. For specific levels of learners – elementary, intermediate, advanced – which approach to teaching listening do you consider the most suitable? Why?
3. Is a monolingual teaching approach, as described in Section 1.3, appropriate all of the time when developing listening skills? Why?
4. When would an integrated approach to teaching listening be most appropriate?

2 Models of Listening

2.1 Introduction

In this chapter, we consider some of the basics in learning to listen. The ability to hear is a natural process that develops in all normal infants. Indeed, most of us begin to hear sounds before we are even born. The physical components of the listening process combine with the cognitive development in a child, resulting in sophisticated listening skills. The natural ability to hear, however, is often mistaken for a fully developed skill that needs no further fine-tuning. As we illustrate, L1 listeners often need training in how to listen just as much as L2 listeners do. Several models have already been developed to account for how we develop listening skills. In this chapter, we review some of these models. We maintain later in the book (Chapter 6), though, that these models are insufficient in themselves to account for all listening processes and that a new model needs to be developed. This new model is briefly previewed.

2.2 Listening Development in the First Language

The process of listening and discriminating what we hear begins before we are even born and develops rapidly during the first year of childhood. Babies in utero have the capacity to listen and discriminate. Studies by De Casper and Spence (1986) demonstrated that unborn babies could be "programmed" to recognize speech patterns. These researchers had expectant mothers read out loud the same short children's story every day for six weeks prior to giving birth. Once born, the infants were played two short stories recorded by their mothers: the one their mother had read out loud each day and another unheard story. The results showed that the newborn infants attended to the story they had heard in utero more than they attended to the new story.

The ability to discriminate sounds at a very early age appears to be evident not only in the mother tongue but in other languages also. For instance, Werker and Tess (1984) found that 6- to 8-month-old and 8- to 10-month-old babies from English-speaking homes could discriminate contrasting sounds in three languages: English, Salish (a North American Indian language), and Hindi. However, the same babies at 12 months had lost this ability in Salish and Hindi and could only discriminate the English sound contrasts. Babies in their first year have also been found to be able to discriminate between the sound of their mother's voice and that of other females (De Casper and Fifer 1980).

There has been extensive research into child aural/oral development, and the stages a child goes through in comprehending and producing language are well known. Owens (1996) outlines some of the aural/oral stages infants go through in the first year of life. According to Owens, a 1-month-old child is able to respond to human voices. By 2 months, the child can distinguish between different types of sound; at 3 months, the ability to turn one's head in response to sounds has developed, and so on until, by the end of the first year, the child can recognize his or her own name.

After the first 12 months, children accelerate their rate of learning and comprehend more and more sophisticated language. By the age of about 3 years, all the English vowels have been acquired, and by about the age of 4 years all of the English consonants are being used. By the age of 7 or 8 years, consonant clusters have been mastered (Owens 1996:95–6). Children are exposed to many hours of language before they are required, or even attempt, to imitate the sounds they hear. Not only are children exposed to many hours of speech, but the speech patterns are also usually repeated over and over again and the complexity of word load is increased, so that children are exposed to language gradually and develop cognitive abilities to deal with it over a period of time. Piaget (1959) was foremost in suggesting how children pass through four cognitive development stages that correspond to their language development levels (cf. Parsons et al. 2001). As children reach different levels of cognitive development, they are able to handle more sophisticated language. There is a huge difference, though, between what children can process and what they can produce. For example, by the age of 6 years, children may know between 8,000 and 14,000 words, yet they will use only a fraction of this vocabulary in their own speech production. The four stages of cognitive development last for years. These years of apprenticeship allow the child to develop complex background knowledge systems with which to match future speech; hence, they develop sophisticated listening skills.

We learn our mother tongue, as children, by listening to it. Then, throughout our lives, listening takes up a substantial proportion of our communication time. According to Burley-Allen (1995), the average time spent on basic skills during the daily communication process is 35 percent for speaking, 16 percent for reading, 9 percent for writing, and 40 percent for listening. However, we are rarely taught how to listen. This has been most obviously illustrated in the workplace where, until recently, company training programs have paid no attention at all to being a "good listener" and instead have focused on other language skills like writing a good memo (Burley-Adams 1995). The question then is, because listening is such an important language skill to develop, and because we use it more than the other language skills, why has such little attention been paid to teaching good listening skills in the L1 context?

Task 1
Consider all the L1 communication situations you have been in today. Make a list of the situations and the language skills you used. Compare your list with a partner. Do they match with the percentages given in the preceding paragraph? Explain to your partner why they might be different.

2.3 Speech Recognition and Short- and Long-Term Memory

To describe the way in which we attend to messages in our first language, a model called the Human Information-Processing System was developed (cf. Bourne, Dominowski, and Coftus 1979). The model explains how we acquire, retain, and retrieve information. Basically, we have three kinds of memory stores: sensory memory, short-term memory, and long-term memory (Figure 2.1).

Auditory messages are first received by the sensory memory from the environment around us. The sensory memory, which detects the signal, is

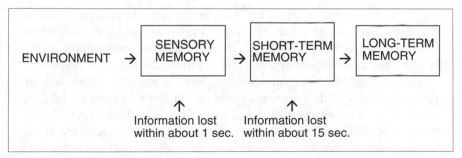

Figure 2.1 The human information-processing system

activated, and the message is held for a period of not more than one second. In this period, the message is held in its exact form. Then, depending on a number of factors, such as the quality of the message, the urgency of the message, and the source of the message, it is either passed on to our short-term memory or lost.

In the short-term memory, we begin to process the message consciously, but we have fewer than 15 seconds to decide what to do with it. We have to decide whether the message contains old or new information. If old information, we check it against what is already held in our long-term memory. If new information, we have to begin to try to match the information with our existing knowledge and make "sense" of the message. If we are able to make sense of the message, then it can be committed to our long-term memory and be fully assessed.

Our long-term memory contains a huge amount of information, and the new message has to be placed within the systems we have developed. In placing the new information, we must make decisions about its usefulness; whether it will be needed again soon, or sometime later; and how to categorize the special syntactic, semantic, and phonological features of the message. Once this is done, we can hold the new message in our long-term memory for as long as we wish.

2.4 Models of the Listening Process

Several models have been developed to explain how the listening process functions in adults. In this chapter, we review the most widely known of these models: the bottom-up model, the top-down model, and the interactive model.

2.4.1 The Bottom-Up Model

The first model of listening to be developed was the bottom-up model. It was developed by researchers working in the 1940s and 1950s. According to the bottom-up model, listeners build understanding by starting with the smallest units of the acoustic message: individual sounds, or phonemes. These are then combined into words, which, in turn, together make up phrases, clauses, and sentences. Finally, individual sentences combine to create ideas and concepts and relationships between them. According to this model, therefore, the different types of knowledge necessary in the listening process are applied in a serial, hierarchical fashion. Bottom-up models of text processing follow a traditional view of communication as

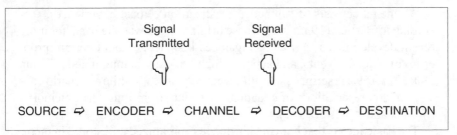

Figure 2.2 A transmission view of communication

the transmission of information. Figure 2.2 (adapted from Shannon and Weaver 1949) is a representation of this model.

According to this model of communication, the sender encodes a message, which passes along the communication channel in the form of a signal and is then decoded by the receiver. Provided that there is no deficiency in the channel and that both the sender and the receiver are using the same code, successful communication is guaranteed. According to this model, communication can take place without any reference to the speaker, hearer, or wider context.

2.4.2 The Top-Down Model

Top-down models emphasize the use of previous knowledge in processing a text rather than relying upon the individual sounds and words. The top-down model was developed when researchers considered the fact that experimental subjects are unable to identify truncated sounds in isolation from the words they form a part of, whereas subjects are quite able to identify truncated words so long as they are presented with the surrounding context. For example, when presented with the sound /mæ/ it is not possible to predict which sound follows it. However, if presented with this sound in a context such as "The cat sat on the /mæ/," then it is quite easy to predict that the following sound is likely to be /t/. This suggests that listeners rely on more than just the acoustic signal to decode a verbal message; they rely on the prior contextual knowledge as well.

In applying contextual knowledge to utterance interpretation, listeners use pre-established patterns of knowledge and discourse structure stored in memory. These pre-established patterns, or "structures of expectation," as Tannen (1979:138), after Ross (1975), refers to them, have been conceived of in a number of ways. Terms used include *schema, frame, script,* and *scenario,* although *schema* is often used as a cover term.

A schema consists of "an active organization of past experiences," according to Bartlett (1932:201), whose original work was the basis for more recent developments. A frame "organizes knowledge about certain properties of objects, events, and action, which typically belong together" (van Dijk 1977:159). A script deals with "event sequences," while a scenario consists of "representations of situations or events from long term memory" (Schank and Abelson 1977).

The basic idea is that human knowledge is organized and stored in memory according to re-occurring events. Schank and Abelson (1977) characterize a restaurant event, or script, as being made up of four "scenes": entering, ordering, eating, and exiting, along with necessary "props" (tables, menu, etc.), roles (customer, waiter, etc.), entry conditions (customer is hungry, customer has money, etc.), and results (customer has less money, customer is less hungry, etc.). Once the structure of an event is stored as a schema in memory, it aids individuals in negotiating future events, in allowing them to predict what is likely to happen. In a similar way, knowledge of previous texts (spoken or written) also aids in negotiating subsequent texts. Thus studies have shown that subjects' levels of comprehension are considerably higher if the subjects are already familiar with the subject matter and/or text type they are presented with than if they have not previously encountered the subject matter or text type. Knowledge of the overall structure and meaning of the text at this macro-level, it is hypothesized, compensates for any problems in understanding microlevel elements, such as sound discrimination, syntax, and word and utterance level semantics. Listening is purpose-driven in this model, and listeners attend to what they need. They only activate those expectations that they deem to be relevant to the text being processed.

2.4.3 The Interactive Model

If listening involves both bottom-up and top-down processing, it follows that some sort of model that synthesizes the two is required. This we have in the so-called interactive model, as developed, most notably, by Rumelhart (1975). According to Rumelhart, whose theory was developed within the context of reading, but which applies equally well to listening, language is processed simultaneously at different levels. In this *parallel processing*, phonological, syntactic, semantic, and pragmatic information interact, although it is not clear exactly how.

Rumelhart sought to demonstrate his hypothesis by having subjects report "on-line" as they read a text. At various points in their reading, subjects were asked to describe their present understanding of the text and, based upon this understanding, what they hypothesized would come next. These hypotheses, or expectations, were then checked against subsequent developments in the text, as noted by the subjects when they continued reading. In this way, Rumelhart demonstrated how readers invoke schemata to make predictions as they read and how these schemata are confirmed or modified as reading (or listening) progresses.

An important advantage of the interactive model over hierarchical models, whether they be bottom-up or top-down, is that it allows for the possibility of individual variation in linguistic processing. From the pedagogic point of view, this opens up the possibility of a model that is sensitive to individual learning styles, on the one hand, and group needs, on the other. At the level of the individual, some individuals may prefer to rely more on top-down processing, while others may favor an approach with more emphasis on bottom-up processes. At the level of the group, beginners are likely to need to spend more time on developing basic bottom-up skills of decoding. For more advanced learners, however, who have mastered basic phonology and syntax, emphasis on the development of top-down skills of applying schematic knowledge may be more appropriate, although even advanced learners need to work on bottom-up features of fast speech (see Chapter 3).

Task 2

Work with a partner. Open a textbook and look for a listening exercise. Does the exercise help develop a bottom-up, top-down, or interactive approach to listening? How do you know?

2.5 Second Language Listeners

Whereas L1 listeners have many hours of passive listening before they seriously need to attend to the messages they hear, L2 listeners are usually not so privileged. In L2 situations, attending becomes part of the active learning process. The processes we use as L2 listeners may be technically somewhat similar to those of L1 situations, but barriers to comprehension and additional processes that L2 listeners must perform can make listening in a second language an arduous task. For instance, suppose that while listening to someone, an aircraft flies overhead. Although this may hamper the sensory memory of both L1 and L2 listeners, L1 listeners may be able to compensate for the disturbance by means of linguistic inference, or cultural background knowledge, and may be able to make sense of what was being said at the time of the noise. On the other hand, an L2 listener may need to hear the full message in order to comprehend it. Once the message is in short-term memory, the L1 listener will be able to access *automatic processing devices* (see Hetherington and Parke 1999). These processes allow the listener to quickly match up the message and decide whether it is worth attending to more in long-term memory. Unless the L2 listener has attained a level whereby these automatic processing devices can be used, the listener needs to rely on *controlled processing*, which requires more attention before any decision on the message can be made. Then again, once the message gets into the long-term memory, the L1 listener has an array of schemata to match the message against. For the L2 listener, the schemata may not be so large or sophisticated, and even if the message is considered important, it may be difficult to retrieve the message once it is in the long-term memory, as the L2 listener may have filed the message in the "wrong" place.

To help L2 learners acquire a high level of listening ability, we need a pedagogical model that accounts for not only the core factors of how listeners process information (top-down, bottom-up, interactive) but also all the other dimensions that may affect the way messages are perceived and processed (see Chapter 6).

Task 3

Before reading any more of this book, try to make a list of any aspects associated with listening that you feel are not accounted for in the models presented earlier: bottom-up, top-down, or interactive.

Task 4

Before reading any more of this book, list ways you think learners can be trained to become better listeners.

2.6 Conclusion

Humans are born with an innate ability to hear. However, hearing is not listening, and many factors need to be considered in the development of effective listening skills. Just as L1 listeners benefit from training in how to listen, L2 learners also need to be trained. Models such as bottom-up, top-down, and interactive processing are at the core of learning listening skills, and most textbooks and current pedagogy for L2 learners take these models into account. We suggest, though, that these models do not go far enough in explaining the complexities of developing effective and efficient listening skills. A range of other factors needs to be taken into account in a pedagogic approach to listening. These factors, or dimensions, as we will refer to them, are illustrated in Figure 6.1. Before presenting this model in detail, however, in the next three chapters we will prepare the ground by dealing with other issues, namely, the different types of meaning involved in effective listening (Chapter 3), the particular features of spoken (as opposed to written) language (Chapter 4), and learning styles and listening strategies (Chapter 5).

2.7 Discussion

1. How does our knowledge of information processing help us to teach listening?
2. In groups, discuss some of the ways in which as L1 listeners we can have problems when listening. What implications does this have when teaching L2 learners?
3. For a group of learners you are familiar with, how do they usually approach developing their listening: by way of bottom-up, top-down, or interactive processing? How do you know?
4. In groups, compare your answers to Tasks 3 and 4. If you were teaching a class for a limited time, say two hours of listening per week for eight weeks, which of the ways you have listed would you try to work into the syllabus?

3 Types of Meaning for Listening

3.1 Introduction

In this chapter, we consider the different types of meaning a model of listening must account for. As listening is a cognitive activity and not susceptible to direct observation, it is very difficult to study and describe. However, as an essential component of communicative competence, it is necessary that we have an idea of what is involved in listening in any attempt to develop a principled approach to language pedagogy. In this chapter, we review the various types of meaning that we hypothesize must form a part of any such model.

3.2 Types of Meaning

In order to comprehend a spoken message, four main types of knowledge may be drawn on: *phonological* – the sound system; *syntactic* – how words are put together; *semantic* – word and propositional knowledge; and *pragmatic* – the meaning of utterances in particular situations. We review these types of meaning in turn, suggesting what role they might play in the overall listening process. In addition, we consider an additional type of meaning, *kinesic* knowledge, which is conveyed by the facial and bodily movement of the speaker. This type of meaning, of course, is present only in those types of listening where the speaker is visible.

3.2.1 Phonological Knowledge

3.2.1.1 PHONEMES

Phonological knowledge is needed in listening comprehension to be able to segment the message into its component sounds. We will start with the *phonemes*, the smallest unit of sound that can distinguish two words. For example, the words *big* and *pig* differ only in their initial sounds,

/b/ and /p/, while the words s*hip* and *sheep* differ in the vowels /ɪ/ and /iː/. /b/, /p/, /ɪ/, and /iː/ are thus all phonemes. So-called Standard or "Received" Pronunciation of British English has 44 phonemes, of which 24 are consonants and 20 are vowels. We would stress, though, that the numbers and classes of phoneme vary among different varieties of English.

Children acquire the full range of phonemes of their L1 early in the language acquisition process. As they listen to the sounds around them, they learn to classify them into prototypical categories, until gradually they come to recognize all sounds as belonging to one of the 44 phonemes. The phonemes in any two languages are never quite the same, so that in learning a new language, learners need to acquire a new set of phonemes. Children under the age of puberty are able to do this remarkably accurately. By the onset of puberty, however, it seems that the brain has programmed all the phonemes it is willing to recognize into a fixed set of categories. Acquiring a new set for an L2 becomes problematic. L2 speakers tend to assimilate the L2 phonemes to their established L1 system. Thus, French speakers of English find it difficult to distinguish between English /ɪ/ and /iː/, conflating the two sounds to approximate to the closest French sound /i/. For French speakers of English, therefore, it is difficult to distinguish between English *ship* /ʃɪp/ and *sheep* /ʃiːp/. Similarly, Spanish speakers of English are usually unable to distinguish English /ʌ/ and /æ/, thus /kæt/ (*cat*) may be pronounced more like /kʌt/ (*cut*). And Arab speakers of English have problems with /p/ and /b/. They have difficulty therefore in distinguishing between such words as *pen* and *ben*.

Task 1

Consider a group of learners you are familiar with. Which phonemes do they usually have problems distinguishing in English? How can you help them better discriminate the sounds?

3.2.1.2 STRESS

Stress, the application of greater force to a syllable, occurs at the level of the word and of the sentence. Every word of more than one syllable will have one syllable that carries the primary stress. Stress is important in speech perception at the word level. In some cases it is the only feature distinguishing between two words, such as 'import (noun) versus im'port (verb).

Word stress tends to be neutralized at the level of the clause or tone group (see following discussion), however, where so-called sentence stress is more significant. When words are combined in clauses, some carry stress, and some do not. Those words that carry stress are usually content words, while destressed words will normally be grammatical, or function, words. Thus, in the following sentence (which consists of two clauses), the stressed words, the content words, are in bold, and the destressed words, the grammatical words, are not.

The **woman went** to the **car**, and her **driver opened** the **door**.

Clearly, stress, in identifying content words, is important for comprehension. Stress patterns give a language its overall *rhythm*. Standard English is said to be one of those languages that tends toward a *stress-timed* rhythm (i.e., stressed syllables tend to occur at regular intervals). In stress-timed languages like English, the unstressed words tend to be spoken more quickly between the stressed words, in order to maintain the overall rhythm. This contrasts with *syllable-timed* languages in which every syllable tends to have the same duration. Other languages that tend to be stress-timed include German, Russian, and Arabic, while syllable-timed languages include French, Spanish, Chinese, and Hungarian. Learners whose L1 is syllable-timed are likely to be challenged by the stress-timed tendency of English, although it is worth pointing out that many of the new varieties of English, such as Indian English and West Indian English, tend to be syllable-timed.

Task 2

Look at the following sentences. On which words would you place the stress? There are different possibilities. How would you demonstrate the stress in the sentences to a class of learners?

1. The man ran away.
2. He gave her a huge bunch of flowers.
3. Martha will give a lecture today.

3.2.1.3 TONE GROUPS

Speech can be divided into tone groups. Tone groups are the basic units of information the speaker wants to convey. Tone groups are often, though not always, equated with clauses. Each tone group will have one syllable that is more heavily stressed and is accompanied by a pitch movement (the *tonic* syllable), thus creating *intonation*. Intonation patterns created through such stress and pitch movement provide important meaning over and above what is contained in the words of an utterance. The tonic signals what is new or important information, while the rest of the tone group contains information that is less prominent because it is already familiar or can be recovered from context. Because it signals the new information, the tonic very often occurs near the end of the tone group, although this is not always the case. Compare the following two examples. In the first statement, the tonic is on the last word because this is the most important part of the message. In the second, however, stress is on the second word because this is the part of the question the speaker wants to emphasize.

A: Mary decided to go to the **cinema**.
B: What **movie** did she see?

L2 learners who are not sensitive to such patterns and who rely overmuch on grammar may misunderstand utterances that depend on intonation for their meaning.

3.2.1.4 ASSIMILATION AND ELISION

One major challenge in teaching foreign or L2 learners of English to decode the phonological system of English is that the features we have reviewed are subject to considerable variation when occurring in actual speech. Standard phonological descriptions of English are usually based on an idealized model derived from single-word or short-sentence citation forms enunciated with great care and precision, what Gillian Brown (1990:158) refers to as English in its "fullest and most explicit form." This is not the language that learners are likely to encounter in real life (although they probably will in their textbooks). "Real" spoken language is simplified (from the speaker's point of view) so that sounds run into one another (*assimilation*) or may be reduced or left out (*elision*). Gillian Brown (1990), in her much more detailed treatment of this question than we have space for here, provides examples of the sort of assimilation and elision that are a normal part of everyday educated speech.

Assimilations

	Full form	**Assimilated form**
1. amount by	/ə'maʊntbaɪ/	[ə'maʊmʔpbaɪ]
2. armoured car	/'ɑːməd'kɑ/	['ɑːməg'kɑ]
3. Mexican games	/'meksɪkən'geɪmz/	['meksɪkəŋ'geɪmz]

Elision

	Elided sound	Full form	Elided form
1. first three	/t/	/fɜːstˈθriː/	[fɜːsˈθriː]
2. suspended from	/d/	/səˈspendɪdfrəm/	[səˈspendɪfrəm]
3. of course	/v/	/əvˈkɔːs/	[əˈkɔːs]
4. already	/l/	/ˈɔːlredɪ/	[ˈɔːredɪ]
5. meeting in Rome	/n/	/ˈmiːtɪŋɪnˈrəʊm/	[ˈmiːtɪŋĩˈrəʊm]

(adapted from Brown 1990:66–77)

Typical of this simplification is the reduction of destressed syllables so that both consonants and vowels are less explicitly pronounced. Among the consonants, for example, fricatives coming in initial syllable position are articulated with less friction than those occurring in syllable final position, and syllable initial plosives have less of an "explosion" of sound than do syllable final plosives. From the vowels, there will be a tendency to reduce to the central shwa /ə/ or /ɪ/ sounds.

One important effect of reductions such as these is that the boundaries between words become blurred. Thus, while *bus stop* would be pronounced /bʌs stɒp/ in its *citation form*, in natural speech it is more likely to occur as /bʌstɒp/. Similarly, *extremely* would be /ɪkˈstrimlɪ/ in citation form, but /ksˈtrimlɪ/ in natural speech (examples from Brown 1990:75–6). While this may not represent a particular problem for a native speaker (ns) who has been brought up to recognize connected speech rather than individual words in isolation, for a nonnative speaker (nns), who has been taught to recognize individual words and short sentences in their idealized citation forms, this may come as a rather nasty shock.

Task 3

Asking learners to practice speech patterns heightens their listening discrimination abilities. Look at the following sentences, which might be used in a speaking/listening exercise. Decide how they would be spoken. Which parts of the sentences would you ask learners to assimilate or elide?

1. Which one do you think is most suitable?
2. Did he give her the pen?
3. I would have come if you had asked me.

For example, for the following question, the first three words are assimilated:

Do you know Mary?
Doyouknow Mary?

3.2.2 Syntactic Knowledge

Language is a generative system. It uses a limited set of combinatorial rules to create an infinite number of possible sentences. The meaning of a sentence cannot be reduced to the sum of the meaning of the words that compose it, and it is the role of syntax to establish the relationships between the words of a sentence and the meanings these relationships carry. The process of the structural analysis of incoming language data is referred to as *parsing*.

If we hear the following two sentences, which contain exactly the same words but in different order, our knowledge of syntax allows us to distinguish their very different meanings:

/subject/	/verb/	/object/
The woman	chased	the girl.
The girl	chased	the woman.

Specifically, in this case, we know that the initial subject position in the English sentence is normally taken up by the *agent*, or "doer" of the action, while the object, or complement, position, following the verb, is normally occupied by the *patient*, or recipient of an action. Thus, in the first sentence, the subject, *the woman*, is the agent and the object, *the girl*, is the patient. In the second sentence, the situation is the reverse, with the subject, *the girl*, as the agent and the object, *the woman*, as the recipient.

As we process incoming messages, the brain applies its knowledge of syntactic rules to parse sentences and make sense of them. It does this, we assume, in two stages: by assigning units (words, phrases, clauses) to the larger units (constituent structures) of which they are a part, on the one hand, and by recognizing the relationships created between the units, on the other. In the following sentence there are three units, or constituent structures: two noun phrases (NP) (*the woman, the ball*) with an intervening verb phrase (VP) (*hit*).

NP	VP	NP
The woman	hit	the ball.

Each NP is made up of an article and a noun, while the VP consists of only one word, a head verb. The constituent structure of this sentence can be represented as follows (where S = sentence):

NP + VP + NP > S

Alternatively, it can be represented by a tree diagram, as follows:

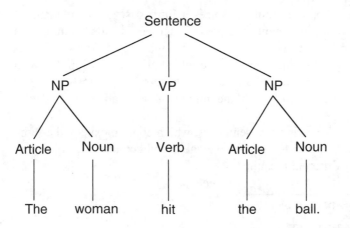

At the second processing stage – interpreting the relationships between the constituents – we apply the rule already employed with our previous example (i.e., that the NP in subject position is the agent, the doer of the action, and that the NP in object position is the patient, or receiver).

This is a minimal account of the sort of syntactic knowledge that we assume to be required in processing incoming speech. We are not sure how this processing is done; some theories suggest that parsing is a purely formal process, independent of other psycholinguistic processes (Chomsky's *universal grammar*, for example), while other *connectionist* theories (theories that claim that many processes take place at the same time in parallel) posit that parsing is intimately related to other cognitive/linguistic processes.

Syntax has traditionally received a lot of attention in second language pedagogy. Indeed, most materials, even today, are organized around the main syntactic patterns of the target language – the so-called structural syllabus. The logic of this is twofold. First, because languages differ in the syntactic patterns of which they are made up, one of the main tasks in learning a foreign language is considered to be the mastery of its (different) syntax. Second, because the syntax of a language can be reduced to a finite set of categories, a structural syllabus can make the organization of teaching systematic.

While we would agree that there is a considerable degree of truth in these principles, we should make a number of observations. First, some languages are more different in their syntax than others. Italian and Spanish, for example, have rather similar syntactic systems. (They both derived historically from the same root language, Latin.) Italian or Spanish and Chinese, however, are very different. In the two Latin languages, syntactic relations are indicated by word inflection. (Such languages are classified as *synthetic*.) In Chinese, however, syntax is coded in independent syntactic form elements. (Such languages are classified as *analytic*.)

The synthetic/analytic dichotomy is just one dimension on which the syntactic "distance" between languages can be compared. Another *typological* variable is word order, the typical ordering of S, V, and O in the simple sentences of the language. English is a SVO language, while Japanese and Turkish are SOV, and Welsh is VSO. However, all possible orders – SOV, SVO, VSO, VOS, OVS, and OSV – occur among the world's languages.

Other basic typologies applying to languages have also been identified, such as whether they are *agglutinative* (i.e., they attach separable affixes to roots so that a word may consist of a root plus several affixes) and whether they are *adpositional* or *postpositional* (i.e., whether they use mainly prepositions – English: *for the man* – or postpositions – Turkish: *the man for*). On all of these dimensions, languages can be closer syntactically or further apart.

Task 4

Consider a language, other than English, with which you are familiar. What is the typical sentence ordering of the language? Make a list of the problems this causes students who are learning English.

Another point we would make is that although syntax is important in establishing meaning, it is not always absolutely essential. In many situations, failure to discriminate syntactic features can be compensated for by other factors. Lexis, or vocabulary, of course, is vital, and studies have shown that understanding is more dependent on the discrimination of key lexical items than syntactic forms and relationships. If we hear the sentence *The girl hit the ball over the fence*, even if we understand only the key words – *girl . . . hit . . . ball . . . fence* – we have a fairly good idea of what this sentence means. Phonology may also compensate for syntactic failure. A rising intonation pattern, for example, may be sufficient for recognizing a question, without the need to discriminate the interrogative syntactic form that often accompanies it. Furthermore, listeners may use inferences where they fail to discriminate syntax. For example, we hear the following exchange:

A: Do you like the car or the motor-bike?
B: The motor-bike.

Even if we do not understand the syntax of the interrogative of the question, as long as we understand the individual words, by retrospective inference – that B is accepting what must have been some sort of request or offer – we can infer that A asked a question.

In addition, fortunately for listeners, the syntax of spoken language tends to be simpler than that of written text. Written language, as we shall see, tends to use more complex syntactic structures than does spoken language. Spoken language tends to consist of simple clauses or clause fragments linked together, whereas written language tends to employ more complex sentences, with complex noun groups, coordination, and subordination. (See Chapter 4).

Finally, however, concerning the finite nature of syntactic categories and rules, we would point out that although the categories and rules may be finite, the uses to which these categories and rules may be put, that is, their possible meanings, are infinite. The basic use of the present simple tense in English is in describing states of affairs:

Hot air rises.

But it can also be used to describe actions. A soccer commentator, for example, might say:

X passes to Y.

Or in storytelling, a speaker might say:

So she says to me . . .

In the latter two cases, the present tense is being used to refer to past actions. Similarly, the present continuous tense can refer to future actions: "I'm playing tennis tomorrow."

3.2.3 Semantic Knowledge

3.2.3.1 SEMANTICS

Semantic knowledge refers to knowledge of the meaning of the words and the meaning of the relations between the words in a sentence. It also refers to the relations between the meanings of the individual sentences making up a discourse. We have already seen that semantic knowledge plays a role in syntactic processing, insofar as understanding of lexical words and the relations of the elements in the sentence (agent, patient, etc.) is also necessary for that process. In normal sentence processing, indeed, semantic considerations tend to dominate understanding, while syntax plays a minor role in confirming any problematic semantic relations where necessary. In one study, for example, subjects were presented with sentences spoken at various speeds. In sentences spoken at slower speeds, both semantics and syntax had effects on comprehension, whereas only the semantics mattered at faster speeds (French 1981, reported in Taylor 1990:129–30).

In line with this dominance of semantics over syntax, what tends to endure in individuals' memories after processing sentences is not the linguistic form but the semantic content. Mental representations of semantic meaning at the sentence level are referred to as *propositions*. A proposition is taken as the smallest unit of meaning to which we can assign a truth value (i.e., it can be said to be either true or false).

3.2.3.2 PROPOSITIONAL HIERARCHIES

In addition to its role in the processing of individual words and sentences, semantic knowledge is required in building up propositional hierarchies, that is, in establishing the relationships between the propositions in a text and putting them into a coherent order. Relationships between propositions are established by *co-reference*, the recurrence of sentence components. Recognition of co-referencing requires knowledge of surface level *cohesion* and underlying *coherence*. Cohesion refers to the formal links that mark various types of interclausal relations. The major types of cohesion (Halliday and Hasan 1976; Halliday 1994) follow:

Reference – referring back to an item with a personal pronoun, possessive pronoun, demonstrative pronoun, definite article, and the like (see Halliday 1994:312ff):

- His wife was waiting at the station. He went and met *her*. (personal pronoun)
- He went to the hospital and saw *his* sick grandmother. (possessive pronoun)
- The bag was very heavy. *The* weight was due to the potatoes. (definite article)

Ellipsis – omission of words that can be presupposed:

- Are you going to the movie? Yes (I am going to the movie).

Substitution – omission of words similar to ellipsis, but with an element holding the place of the missing words:

- She said she would kill him and she *did* (kill him).

Conjunction – use of linking words to show logical relations (e.g., *and, but, therefore*).

- Mary went to the market *and* returned home.

Lexical reiteration – repetition of the same word or substitution of a word similar in meaning (exact repetition, synonyms, near synonyms, and superordinates [general classes] and hyponyms [subcategories]):

- Susan likes science. *Science* is her best subject at school. (exact repetition)
- John's father works in a mine. He goes down the *pit* every day. (synonym)
- The fog came down very quickly. She had never seen such thick mist before. (synonym)
- He likes all sorts of *fruit*, but *mango* and *papaya* are his favorites. (superordinate *fruit* and hyponyms *mango, papaya*)

Coherence refers to the underlying relations that link clauses or propositions. It is not a formal property of texts, but of the meaning relations perceived by speakers and hearers based on their knowledge and logic. Various models have been put forward for coherence. One model that can account for a large number of texts is the clause relational model of Hoey (1983). Hoey identifies two fundamental relations between clauses: *logical sequence* and *matching*. Logical sequence would include *phenomenon-reason, cause-consequence*, and *instrument-achievement* relations:

- Water evaporates when the temperature rises. (phenomenon-reason)
- John got wet in the rain. He went up to change his clothes. (cause-consequence)
- They paid a high price. They got what they wanted. (instrument-achievement)

Matching occurs when segments of text are compared or contrasted. It includes *contrast* and *compatibility*:

- She is intelligent. He is stupid. (contrast)
- Terrorists are a great problem in the Middle East. The same is true in Southeast Asia. (compatibility)

Another model is put forward by Crombie (1985a, 1985b).

3.2.4 Pragmatic Knowledge

Research into syntax and semantics is typically done using the sentence as the basic unit. Sentences are units of written discourse, and one can call into question the applicability of such a unit as a model for spoken text comprehension. According to Halliday (1989, 1994), spoken language is made up of complex chains of clauses, clauses being roughly equivalent, as we have seen, to tone groups. These clausal structures of spoken language are much more complex than for written language. If one looks at a transcription of spoken language, one will usually find that it is replete with false starts, repetitions, and clause fragments, in addition to a range of *paralinguistic* features (*ums* and *ahs*). Complete sentences are often the exception rather than the rule in spoken language, especially in casual conversation. People have no particular difficulty in comprehending spoken language, however. Indeed, there are a number of reasons for considering speech as the primary form of language (Clark 1996:11): It is universal (unlike written language, where many languages do not have a written form and many people are not able to read), it requires no formal instruction (unlike written language), and it is the form in which one acquires one's first language. If syntactic sentences are the exception rather than the rule in conversational language, this suggests a reduced role for syntax in comprehension. As we have already seen, even at the sentence level, semantics tends to dominate syntax. But another level also plays an important role in comprehension – *pragmatics*.

Pragmatics is concerned with the meaning and use of language in specific situations. The unit of analysis in pragmatics is not the sentence, but the *utterance*, which we can define here as the specific linguistic realization of a proposition in a given situation. An important role for pragmatics is in the disambiguation of utterances. If we take in isolation a simple utterance such as *Okay* out of context, this expression can have many meanings. Perhaps its most common meaning is agreement. This would be the interpretation in the following exchange:

A: Can I borrow your pen?
B: Okay.

However, in the context of an academic lecture, a professor might say the following:

Okay, let's move on to the next section.

The function of *okay* here would seem to be to indicate that the professor has arrived at a point in the lecture where a given topic has been completed (and it is therefore possible to move on to the next one). Then again, take another exchange:

A: How did you do in the exam?
B: Okay.

Here the meaning of *okay* is something like "not bad and not good."

One aspect of context, then, is topic, what the ongoing discourse is about, its subject matter. But context comprises a whole range of features, all of which may play a role in the interpretation of an utterance. Hymes (1972) produced an inventory of contextual parameters that may affect meaning by means of an acrostic, SPEAKING, as follows:

Setting	time and place
Participants	addressor, addressee, audience
Ends	ends in view; an outcome of the discourse
Act characteristics	the form and content of what is said
Key	tone, manner, and spirit in which the utterance is produced
Instrumentalities	channel and code or subcode
Norms	of interaction and interpretation
Genres	traditional categories of speech events

We will examine just a few of these parameters to show how they may work. Starting with setting (place), the following exchange occurred in the context of arranging a time for a meeting. With only this context, it is difficult to work out what the speaker intended with this utterance:

A: When can we have a meeting?
B: Tomorrow's Friday.

This exchange was in fact produced in the presence of one of the authors in a Middle Eastern university. Once we know this geographical context, we can put a specific interpretation on it. What the speaker actually meant was that a meeting would not be possible (because in the Middle East, Friday is not a working day).

In terms of the contextual parameter of instrumentality (channel), how are we to interpret the following?

two, seven, three, five, seven, nine

In isolation, it is just a string of meaningless numbers. If we know that these numbers were uttered through the speech channel of the telephone, then they may be interpreted as a case of speaker self-identification.

Our third contextual parameter example is participant (addressee). If the following utterance were addressed to a group of soldiers, then it could be interpreted as an order to line up:

Fall in!

On the other hand, when addressed to a group of children standing by a swimming pool, it would have a more literal meaning.

Task 5

Consider the following utterances and decide on the contexts in which they might be heard:

1. Go left!
2. Tomorrow's fine.
3. I'll do it myself.
4. Close it.

Moving now to the last dimension of Hymes's model, genre, if we take an academic research article, it has been shown that this genre follows very stereotypical patterns. Another stereotypical genre is the sales letter. Some genres are so conventionalized that the language used is always exactly the same. Coronations would be such an example. Certain genres, on the other hand, may be of a more hybrid nature. In his study of political language, Fairclough (1992) has noted, for example, how such discourse may exhibit features of formal political language, on the one hand, but at the same time contain features of conversational language. Fairclough describes this as the "mixing of the language of face to face interaction with the language of mass communication" (p. 90).

In producing utterances, speakers must estimate how much of the contextual knowledge addressees are likely to be able to bring to bear in interpreting what they say. Utterances, therefore, always carry varying degrees of *presupposition*. The role of hearers in utterance interpretation is to use contextual knowledge to work out what is presupposed. Obviously, there is a lot of room for misunderstanding here because speakers and hearers never know exactly what the state of mutual knowledge is. On the other hand, in L2 situations, contextual knowledge can make up for lack of phonological, syntactic, and semantic discrimination. The more familiar interlocutors are with each other, other things being equal, the less chance there is for misunderstanding. At the same time, however, if interlocutors know each other well, they are likely to make greater presuppositions, thus incurring a greater danger of misunderstanding. The following conversational exchange seems to have no meaning whatsoever:

A: Where's my book?
B: I haven't been to America.
A: Oh, okay.

However, the conversation makes perfect sense when we know that it occurred between two teachers, one of whom was going to attend a conference in the United States and had offered to pick up a copy of a book for the other teacher.

In addition to using context as a guide to the pragmatic interpretation of utterances, it has been argued that speakers and hearers operate on a system of *interpretive principles*, or *maxims*. Grice (1975) argued that hearers apply four maxims in the interpretation of utterances: the maxims of *quantity, quality, relevance*, and *manner*. The maxim of quantity tells hearers that a contribution can be expected to be as informative as necessary for the purposes of the exchange, but it should supply no more information than is necessary; the maxim of quality indicates that a message will normally state the truth; the maxim of relevance promises that what is said is likely to be relevant to the ongoing conversation; and the maxim of manner indicates that an utterance will under normal circumstances be clear, orderly, and unambiguous. Sperber and Wilson (1986) have reduced Grice's maxims to just one principle: *relevance*, the idea that any utterance can be interpreted on the basis that it is presumed to be relevant to the ongoing communication.

In both Grice's and Sperber and Wilson's models, listeners presume that communication is cooperative, on the one hand, and they will look for the most efficient way of processing an utterance's meaning in terms of the maxims or principle, on the other. If, after attempting to process the meaning of an utterance according to the maxims or principle, meaning is not clear, then listeners will look for alternative readings. Indirect meanings, such as irony, metaphor, and *indirect speech acts*, are thus comprehended as such when listeners realize that the maxims are being flouted and that alternative, nonliteral meanings are intended.

To take an example of irony, imagine a situation where a mother, having asked her son to tidy up his room, finds the job not to have been well done, but says the following:

You've really done a good job there!

The situation here suggests the mother is flouting the maxim of quality – be truthful – because the room is in fact still untidy. The child, aware of this state of affairs, will thus infer that the mother is being ironic in her statement and is in fact criticizing, not praising.

Although most scholars agree that Grice's cooperative framework is universal, many believe that different maxims operate differently according to cultures. Thus, it has been argued, in some Asian countries, there is a maxim of politeness, which is more important than the maxim of quality and quantity; it is more important in these societies, it is argued, to maintain good relations than to be absolutely truthful or concise. If one takes a broad definition of culture to refer to any social group, then the principles of communication can be seen to vary according to situation. The maxim of quality (truthfulness), for example, is clearly applied differently by politicians in their speeches on the election hustings from the way it is applied by witnesses in a court of law.

To conclude this section, one needs to go beyond the information-processing model presented in Chapter 2 to take account of indirect meaning and different meanings according to different cultures.

Task 6

Look at the following conversational exchanges. Apply whatever aspects of Hymes's SPEAKING acronym you consider appropriate to make sense of them.

1. A: You know my John?
   B: Yeh.
   A: Well, he likes cheese.
2. A: How are you?
   B: I've just taken two Panadol.
   A: Oh, good.
3. A: Can you see anything?
   B: Dolphins!
   A: I'll get us some more coins.

3.2.5 Kinesic Knowledge

Kinesic knowledge is knowledge about the meaning of nonverbal means of communication, such as facial expression, eye contact, and body movement and positioning. Kinesic meaning adds support or shades of meaning to what people say. Indeed, in some situations, nonlinguistic messages, such as a shrug or a nod, may be all that is needed to convey a speaker's meaning without any actual words. Kinesic meanings vary across cultures and languages. For example, in some cultures, a shake of the head means "no," while in some other cultures it means "yes." Different cultures also have different conventions about the degree of proximity that is appropriate between speakers and the amount of physical contact (if any) that is acceptable. Unfortunately, there is no agreed system for describing kinesic meaning, and therefore teaching it in a systematic fashion is problematic. One thing that is worth pointing out, however, is that the typical reliance on audio recordings for the teaching of listening comprehension reduces the exposure of learners to kinesic meaning. Greater use of video and real-life interaction, on the other hand, provides learners with exposure to this important dimension of meaning.

3.3 Conclusion

This chapter examined the essential types of meaning that any model of listening must accommodate. We briefly reviewed the five types of knowledge under the headings of phonology, syntax, semantics, pragmatics, and kinesics. In various communicative situations, one of these types of meaning may play a more dominant role in conveying the message. However, an understanding of each of them is important for successful comprehension.

3.4 Discussion

1. How do you know when students are using semantic knowledge more than syntactic knowledge? What weighting would you give to each when preparing learners for listening?
2. Which aspects of Hymes's SPEAKING inventory do you consider more important than the others when processing information? If you were preparing learners for listening to public announcements, which aspects of the inventory would you focus on and draw the learners' attention to? Why?
3. Consider a group of learners you are familiar with. Which types of knowledge do they have most problems with: phonological, syntactic, semantic, or pragmatic? Why do they have problems?

4 The Nature of Spoken Language

4.1 Introduction

In the previous chapter, we outlined how different types of meaning had to be accounted for in any model of listening comprehension. In this chapter, we focus on the need to consider different types of text.

One common approach in preparing second language learners for listening comprehension is for the teacher to focus on examples of written text and then expect the learners to transfer this knowledge when interpreting spoken texts. For example, a teacher may ask the learners to read a series of questions, listen to a taped recording of a scripted text, and then write answers to the questions. The focus, in this case, is as much on interpreting written text as it is on listening comprehension. As we illustrate in this chapter, spoken and written texts are very different and need to be taught in different ways. In addition to this, much of the listening practice that takes place in the classroom context focuses learners on large chunks of information (similar to a lecture), whereas in real life we do most of our listening in conversational settings. Conversations have very special features that are all too often neglected in second language classrooms.

Notwithstanding the importance of conversation and the emphasis on scripted text in classroom listening activities, spoken text itself can take many forms. For example, it can be distinguished in two broad ways: the type of information given and the amount of time taken. A lecture is an example of what Brown and Yule (1983) identify as *transactional* language (giving information) and is usually characterized by the speaker having *long turns*. A conversation, on the other hand, is usually identified as mostly *interactional* (maintaining social contact), with each speaker having a number of *short turns*. We will look at both types of spoken language in this chapter.

4.2 Speech Versus Writing

Most spoken text differs in many ways from written text; therefore, the object of listening is different from that of reading. A comparison of a transcribed spoken text and a written text is likely to reveal a number of significant differences. Spoken text is *fragmented* (loosely structured) and *involved* (interactive with the listener). Written text, on the other hand, is *integrated* (densely structured) and *detached* (lacking in interaction with the listener). These functional distinctions are realized in certain linguistic features (Figures 4.1a and 4.1b).

As already suggested, spoken and written texts are not two isolated categories, however. Different spoken and written genres can be situated along a continuum marking different degrees of "spokenness" and of "writtenness" and exhibiting to a greater or lesser extent the linguistic features listed in Figures 4.1a and 4.1b. Casual conversation would be at one extreme of spokenness, while academic papers might be at the other extreme of writtenness. Other genres – radio news broadcasts, academic lectures, formal

---

Linguistic Features of Spoken Text

- phonological contractions and assimilations
- hesitations, false starts, and filled pauses
- sentence fragments rather than complete sentences
- structured according to tone units rather than clauses
- frequent occurrence of discourse markers at beginning or end
- tone groups
- high incidence of questions and imperatives
- first and second person pronouns
- deixis (reference outside the text)

Figure 4.1a Distinctive linguistic features of spoken text

Linguistic Features of Written Text

- longer information units
- complex relations of coordination and subordination
- high incidence of attributive adjectives
- wider range and precise choice of vocabulary
- high lexical density (nominalization)
- longer average word length
- more frequent use of passive voice
- high use of coherence and cohesive devices

Figure 4.1b Distinctive linguistic features of written text

ceremonies (e.g., marriages), and the like for spoken language, and business letters, novels, personal letters, and so on for written language – would be situated at different points along the continuum. It might even be the case that some spoken texts (e.g., news broadcasts) are more "written" than some written texts (e.g., postcards or e-mail messages).

Ochs (1979) suggests that the positioning of various genres along the spoken/written continuum depends, at least in part, on the degree to which the language of a given genre is *planned* or *unplanned*. Clearly, casual conversation is unplanned, while academic papers are carefully planned. Academic lectures, on the other hand, are less spontaneous than casual conversation but more spontaneous than academic papers.

Task 1

Look at the continuum of spokenness and writtenness. Place the following genres at their appropriate place on the scale. Compare your ideas with those of a partner.

|--|

spokenness   writtenness

casual conversation	university lecture	academic research article
school textbook	shopping list	postcard
political speech	e-mail message	church service
press conference	telephone travel reservation	radio news

To examine these differences, we will consider the following example of two texts that present basically the same information. The first text is taken from a biology textbook; the second is from a lecture that was part of a course that used the biology textbook (Roberts 1986) as its text.

Text Extract A – Book

CLASSIFICATION AND DIVERSITY OF ORGANISMS

Approximately 1.5 million species of living organisms have been described, and it is estimated that a further three million, and possibly as many as ten million, remain to be discovered. With so many organisms in the world it is important to be able to classify them so as to bring order out of chaos. Classifying things is a basic feature of all human activity which we acquire in early childhood, and it comes as naturally to a biologist as to anyone else. The science of biological classification is known as taxonomy.

Information Units in the Above Text

1. Approximately 1.5 million species of living organisms have been described.
2. An estimated three million to ten million species of living organisms remain to be discovered.
3. The large number of living organisms makes it important to classify them.
4. Classification of the large number of living organisms will bring order out of chaos.
5. Classifying things is a basic feature of all human activity.
6. The activity of classification is acquired in early childhood.
7. Biologists develop the activity of classification as naturally as other people.
8. The science of biological classification is known as taxonomy.

Text Extract B – Lecture (*Key: / =* pause)

Today's lecture then / is on the classification of animals and plants / classification / now there are a huge number of different organisms / living organisms / in the world / no one knows how many there are / well / hold your horses / there are a huge number of different organisms / and so far one and a half million / have been described to science / have been scientifically described / in other words one and a half million organisms have been given a scientific name / and have had descriptions / detailed descriptions / published by scientists / and one and a half million is a huge number of organisms / now there are many many more organisms which have not yet been described scientifically / we only know about a certain number of organisms / and there are many more which we have not yet described and given names to / and because we haven't described them and no one's described them / no one's given them names / we don't know how many there are / but it's not known how many living organisms there are that have not been described scientifically / and there's somewhere probably between three to ten million . . .

Information Units in the Above Text

1. There are a huge number of living organisms in the world.
2. It is not known how many living organisms there are in the world.
3. One and a half million living organisms have been described scientifically.
4. There are many more living organisms that have not been described scientifically.
5. It is not known how many living organisms there are that have not been described scientifically.
6. It is estimated that there are between three million and ten million living organisms that have not been described scientifically.

Looking at these two texts, we see that they present basically the same information. We can schematize this information by breaking the text down into units of information. The written text has eight units of information, compared with six for the spoken text. In spite of containing less information, however, the spoken text has more than twice as many words as the written text (202, compared with 96 for the written text). How can we account for these differences? One thing that we immediately notice is the amount of repetition in the spoken text. The speaker is providing a lot of redundancy to make sure that his listeners (nonnative speakers) grasp what he is saying. Listening is a short-lived activity and, unlike readers, listeners cannot control the speed with which they process the text. Nor can they backtrack to make sure that they have understood correctly. For this reason, speakers often repeat or rephrase parts of their message in order to facilitate comprehension. A second difference between the two texts is that the written text has a much higher *lexical density*. Lexical density is the ratio of content words (nouns, verbs, adjectives, adverbs) to grammatical words (prepositions, auxiliary verbs, conjunctions). In the written text, the content words are close together, whereas in the spoken text they are spaced out by the insertion of a greater number of grammatical words. A third point to be noted is the absence of punctuation in the spoken text. Punctuation is replaced by pauses, as indicated by slashes (/) in the transcription. The positioning of these pauses is essential for comprehension because, together with stress and intonation (see Chapter 3), the pauses indicate how the units of information (the tone units) are structured and hence should be processed.

One conclusion that might be drawn from this comparison is that written text is much more efficient at conveying information. And a further conclusion might be that it would be better if we just wrote everything down! But this is to assume that listening is concerned only with the decoding of information. Spoken language has the potential for much more emotional nuance, contextual sensitivity, personal weighting, interactive hooks, and reference to the real world outside the text. This makes it more engaging and entertaining and explains why people often prefer to listen than to read. We will turn to some of these aspects in the Chapter 6, where we present our pedagogic model of listening. But before that we will consider some of the specific features of conversational listening.

4.3 Conversational Listening

Task 2

Record a three- or four-minute conversation with one or two friends. Choose a topic such as asking about personal matters or your favorite movies. Transcribe the conversation in preparation for the tasks that follow in this section. Or use the transcribed conversation in Section 4.6.

The example we have been looking at is of monologue. Although monologue is an important type of spoken text (particularly in the academic context, where the lecture still reigns supreme), most spoken language takes the form of conversation.

Listening, in the context of conversation, is clearly not just a psycho-perceptual process, as the models outlined in Chapter 2 might lead one to believe. It is also a very social activity, in which both speaker and hearer affect the nature of the message and how it is to be interpreted. Grice's maxims, as we saw in Chapter 2, are based on the assumption of mutual cooperation in conversation. Indeed, in analyzing conversation, it is not easy to talk about "speaker" and "listener," as both interlocutors (in a canonical dyadic exchange) take on both roles.

Concerning the specific listening roles in conversation, a number of activities can be distinguished, in addition to the psychoperceptual processing of the speaker's message. These are recognizing stages in the conversation, topic shift, back-channeling, reformulation, repair, turn-taking, and negotiating meaning and exploiting ambiguity (Clark 1996).

4.3.1 Recognizing Stages in the Conversation

One important activity that listeners perform is facilitating the mutual performance of the different sections in conversation. Conversations can be broken down into three major stages: *openings*, *closings*, and *topics*. In opening a conversation, there must be an initiator, or speaker, but there must also be an interlocutor, or listener. The initiator may begin with a *summons*. The role of the listener is to respond to the summons. Let us take a hypothetical case of a speaker, Susan, and a listener, John. Susan begins with a summons, "John?" John's response, as the listener, to Susan's summons is crucial in deciding the direction the conversation will take. He may respond with a simple "Yes?" In that case, he will be signaling that the opening is successful and that Susan can now introduce a topic of her choice (although he will still be able to reject her chosen topic if he does not like it). On the other hand, he may ignore Susan's summons. Her opening will have been unsuccessful, and no conversation will ensue. As another alternative, he may signal a provisional acceptance of the opening, with something like "What do you want?" Continued conversation will then be conditional on the nature of the topic Susan introduces.

Closings are also important in conversations. A listener's inability to pick up when the speaker is wanting to close the conversation can lead to an embarrassing situation. For example:

A: Well, nice talking to you.
B: Yes, it's been lovely. We must do this again.
A: Well, I really must go now.
B: Where are you going?
A: Oh, I have to get something from the supermarket.
B: That's nice. I'll come with you.
A: Oh, er . . . well, actually, I have to go to the bank first.

Task 3

Identify the sections in your recorded conversation (or in Section 4.6). With a partner, compare what you think the openings and closings are. (There may be more than one.)

4.3.2 Topic Shift

With respect to topics, which make up the main body of a conversation, the listener plays an important role in determining when the conversation will move from one topic to another, a process known as *topic shift*. The role of the listener is to identify points in the discourse when it is appropriate to move on to a new topic. At various points in the ongoing discourse, listeners have the opportunity to take turns at speaking. At such points, they may decide to take a turn or allow the current speaker to continue. If they take a turn, they may choose between continuing with the current topic or switching to a new one. The important thing from the listener's point of view is that the shift must be appropriate. In the following example, A shifts the topic from newspapers to stamps when the transaction for the newspaper has been completed (at least partially).

A: I'd like this newspaper, please.
(pause)
B: There you are. (hands over newspaper)
A: Do you sell stamps?

Although it is not known exactly how listeners judge when a topic shift is appropriate, we may easily recognize when it is not appropriate. This explains why people are sometimes accused of "changing the subject" when speakers consider that the current topic has not been completed, as in the following exchange:

Mother: Have you done your homework?
Child: I think I'll watch TV now.

Task 4
Try to identify any topic shifts in your recorded conversation (or in Section 4.6). With a partner, decide how appropriate these topic shifts are in the development of the conversation. Who initiates the topic shift? Is a speaker deliberately changing the topic? Is there any confusion indicated by the listener(s) because of the topic shift?

4.3.3 Back-Channeling

Another listener activity that affects the structure of conversation is *back-channeling*. In order for speakers to continue with their message, they need signals, or *back-channel cues*, from their listeners to let the speakers know that they are attending. Without back-channel cues, a conversation would likely break down, as the speakers would not know whether the listeners were actively participating in the discourse. This is particularly true with regard to telephone conversations, as speakers may not even know that someone is on the line.

Back-channel cues may be verbal (*yeah, mm, um, ah, of course, oh dear, my God*, etc.) or nonverbal (head nodding, shoulder shrugging, facial gestures and eye gaze, laughter, etc.). Not only are back-channel cues needed to encourage speakers to continue speaking, but they also guide the direction of what is said. A head nod, indicating agreement, is likely to encourage speakers to continue in the same vein. But a shake of the head, indicating disagreement, may cause speakers to modify what they are saying and take a different direction. Back-channel cues may convey a range of attitudes of the listener, including empathy, agreement, disagreement, and indifference; in all cases, however, they affect what speakers say and how they say it.

Task 5

Identify any back-channeling devices used in your recorded conversation (or in Section 4.6). Do the listeners use only one or two types of verbal cues, or do they use a wide range? Do the back-channeling cues vary depending on what is said?

4.3.4 Reformulation

Listeners may also guide a conversation by reformulating speakers' utterances. In this way, listeners clarify for speakers how they are interpreting what is being said. In the following exchange, for example, a professor uses a *reformulation* to interpret what a student is saying and check that his interpretation is in agreement with the intention of the student.

Student: I can't come to see you tomorrow at 9:00 o'clock. I've got a lecture.
Professor: So you want to make the appointment a bit later.
Student: Yes. How about 11:30?

In this example, the professor uses a paraphrase to reformulate what he understands the student to have said. In some cases, however, reformulations may partially or exactly echo the statement they are reformulating. In the next exchange, which is part of a conversation between a university applicant and a professor, the professor repeats exactly the words used by the candidate (although the intonation pattern is different):

Applicant: I got a distinction in my MA dissertation, and I want to go on to MPhil or PhD.
Professor: You got a distinction in your dissertation, and you want to go on to MPhil or PhD. (pause) That would certainly be possible.

Task 6

Identify any reformations in your recorded conversation (or in Section 4.6). Does the listener use exactly the same words as the speaker, or not?

4.3.5 Repair

One way in which listeners may alter the direction a speaker is taking is by correcting misunderstandings, inaccuracies, or errors, referred to as *repair*. In the following example, which took place in a restaurant, A asks to take a chair from an adjoining table, which is unoccupied. Perhaps because A uses the polite formula "Do you mind?" – which would require a negative to indicate agreement – he/she is taken aback at what is an apparent blunt refusal. Realizing that there is a misunderstanding, A clarifies by paraphrasing the original question without using the "Do you mind?" formula. The repair is successful, as this time there is no doubt that B is in agreement.

A: Do you mind if I take this chair?
B: Yes.
A: Eh . . . I mean, may I take it?
B: Yes.

Task 7

Identify any repairs used in your recorded conversation (or in Section 4.6). Why do the repairs occur? What has been misunderstood?

4.3.6 Turn-Taking

Successful performance of listener intervention strategies such as staging, back-channeling, reformulation, and repair depends on the ability of listeners to judge at what point to use them. To ascertain this, listeners need to be familiar with the conventions of *turn-taking*: how interlocutors take turns at speaking and listening. Turn boundaries, rather obviously, are marked when one speaker stops talking and another takes over, although there may be some overlap. However, listeners do not wait until a speaker stops talking before deciding to take a turn. If this were the case, there would be pauses between turns, and studies have shown that speaker switches are usually accomplished with little or no pause at all. Listeners therefore must project forward to the completion of a speaker's turn, which will allow them to intervene. Sacks, Schegloff, and Jefferson (1974), who developed a system of rules for turn-taking, refer to the point at which it is possible for a turn switch to occur as a *transition relevance point*. Listeners rely on a variety of cues to project forward to transition relevance points (Clark 1996:322). These include eye gaze, gestures, syntax, and intonation. Speakers usually tend to direct their gaze away from listeners during a turn and to refocus on the listeners as they finish the turn. (Listeners, in contrast, usually monitor speakers throughout their turns in order to pick up on the signals for the transition relevance point.) Gestures that speakers have been making to accompany their talk tend to be finished, and they tend to relax their bodies. At the end of a turn, the final syllable may be lengthened, accompanied by a falling intonation.

Task 8

Count the number of turns each speaker has in your recorded conversation (or in Section 4.6). Does anyone dominate the conversation? Is there any reason why one speaker should dominate? What are some of the transition devices you notice when speakers change? Discuss your findings with a partner.

4.3.7 Negotiating Meaning and Exploiting Ambiguity

Finally, a listener influences the progress of a conversation by negotiating the meaning to be assigned to an utterance and exploiting ambiguity when it occurs. Although a speaker will usually have a particular intention in making an utterance, it is up to the listener to decide whether that intention, or meaning, is taken up. Thomas (1995:198) cites two exchanges that show how listeners may interpret the same statement in different ways and thereby influence the structure of the ongoing conversation:

Example A

David: Tea or coffee?
Jenny: Coffee, please.

Example B

David: Tea or coffee?
Jenny: Yes, please.
David: Coffee?
Jenny: Thank you.

In example A, the listener, Jenny, interprets David's utterance as an offer to provide her with whichever drink she chooses. In example B, she interprets it as a question as to whether she wants a drink or not (whether it be tea or coffee). In example A, the way Jenny interprets David's initial utterance results in just one exchange to resolve David's invitation. In example B, however, because Jenny interprets David's same statement differently, two exchanges are necessary.

In the following exchange, in which a wife enquires about what her husband would like as a dessert, the husband/listener reads perhaps more into the speaker's question than the latter intended (perhaps the honeydew melon was particularly good or perhaps it needed to be eaten).

Wife: Do you want honeydew melon?
Husband: Why?
Wife: No particular reason, I just thought you might like some.

What these examples show is that meaning is negotiable and that it may take a considerable stretch of discourse before a speaker's meaning becomes clear. Just how long a negotiation takes is dependent, to a great extent, on the role of the listener.

Task 9
Identify any ambiguities in your recorded conversation (or in Section 4.6). Why is there ambiguity? How is it resolved?

4.4 Conclusion

In this chapter, we have highlighted some of the differences between spoken and written text. Spoken text and written text, in their canonical forms, are very different. Therefore, the approaches we have in interpreting each must also be different. Conversation is one of the most important kinds of spoken text, and it is susceptible to cross-cultural and cross-linguistic variation. Back-channeling, reformulating, repairing, taking turns, negotiating meaning, recognizing sections, shifting topics, and exploiting ambiguity are doubtless universal to all languages and cultures. However, in the way they are applied, there is considerable variation. They are therefore features that merit particular attention as a part of second language listening pedagogy.

4.5 Discussion

1. Look at Figures 4.1a and 4.1b. What are the implications for teaching comprehension of spoken text?
2. Have you ever attended a lecture where the professor read out the lecture notes? How difficult was it to comprehend the lecture? What problems did you have? How would you advise the professor on giving a better lecture?
3. What balance do you think there should be between preparing learners for interactional and transactional language and long and short turns with reference to different levels of learners.
4. How did the tasks in this chapter make you more aware of the features of spoken text? How could you use this information when teaching? Discuss the advantages and disadvantages of using such information with your learners. Specify the type of learners you are talking about.

Appendix

4.6 Transcription

Setting: University Staff Common Room, Hong Kong.* Three Western colleagues meet over coffee and chat during their break.

Cultural note. Chinese (or Lunar) New Year is an important festival in Chinese heritage cultures. It is the custom to distribute Lai See packets (red envelopes) containing money to children, unmarried young people, and service workers. A lychee is a small fruit commonly found in mainland China and Hong Kong.

R = Richard   G = Gillian   P = Peter
/ = short pause   // = long pause   indentation = two people speaking at the same time

1. P: Oh hi Gi Gillian/ how's it going?
   (Gillian pours herself some coffee)
2. G: Ehm/ you know/ the word that we always use around here / busy.
3. R: I'm tired of that word.
4. G: Yeah, I hate that word myself// busy.
5. P: What do you mean you can't be *that* busy/ it's near the end of semester.
6. G: What?!
7. R: That's the busiest time!
8. P: You should be winding down, winding down . . .
9. R: I feel like I'm just winding up with all my students assignments due in/
10. P: Oh if you're marking assignments you can have some of mine if you want . . .
11. R: No thank you.
12. G: How about if we give you some of ours/ Do you want to mark some of those practice teaching portfolios?
13. P: What? You're not doing that course again this semester, are you?
14. G: No I'm not doing that course this semester.
15. P: Oh, oh (laugh). You are . . .
16. G: (laugh)
17. P: My god, I thought it ran itself that course.
18. G: (laughing) Very funny.
19. R: So/ do you have any plans for a holiday this Christmas Gillian?
20. G: Holiday? Christmas? You mean with the workload that we have here do we have those things?
21. R: No, the same with me, I'm just going to stay home.
22. P: You're not going any place?
23. R: No, I've got to finish my dissertation.
24. G: Alright
25. R: Still working on it
26. G: It's important, but you got to take one day off – Christmas Day/ have a good Christmas meal.
27. R: I think I'll probably work a few hours, and then have Christmas.
28. G: Yeah. You know I go to church though.
29. P: Are you, are you staying for Christmas? I thought you'd be going back home.
30. G: No, I don't, I never, because it's too short.
31. P: What the break or the trip?
32. G: Yeah, like the trip to the U.K. is too short! (laugh) To fly all the way home and be jet-lagged, and come back and be jet-lagged again. And you're only there for three or four days. It's too expensive, and it's not worth it.
33. R: Yeah. Mmm. What about Chinese New Year?

34. G: Chinese New Year I stay put also. Again it's too short for me to go home.
35. R: You gotta make reservations early. But when is Chinese New Year this year?

(pause)

36. G: I guess February.
37. P: Beginning of February or something like that?
38. G: But I think the time is too short both Christmas and Chinese New Year, so I tend to stay put. There's lots of things to do. I visit friends and/
39. R: Chinese New Year is quite nice. They have those lovely flower markets . . .
40. G: Oh, I love the flower markets . . .
41. R: You can get any type of flower you want . . .
42. G: But the thing I like about the Chinese New Year is the expression on peoples' faces. People are so happy, especially the children. It's what you would find in the West during Christmas. It's the same thing that you see here during Chinese New Year/ And the kids get excited over their Lai See packets.
43. P: What's a lychee packet?
44. G: (laugh) You don't know what a Lai See packet is?
45. R: Yeah, you get lychees in them.
46. G/R: (laughing)
47. R: Well that's okay. We don't have to give him one.
48. G: Just walk around and talk to kids and say, "How many Lai See packets do you have?"
49. P: So what's the problem about not being married?
50. R: Well you don't have to give them, but you get them.
51. G: Yeah, but you don't know what it is so we're not going to give you one.
52. R: Yeah, we'll give you a packet with lychees in them. (laugh)
53. G: (laugh)
54. P: Oh gosh, look at the time I've got another class, better get going.
55. G: Okay, yeh I've got more marking to do. Good to see you guys.
56. R: Yeah, see you later. Don't work too hard.
57. G/P: Bye.

5 *Learning Styles and Listening Strategies*

5.1 Introduction

To teach effective listening we must be aware of how our students approach their learning in general and how they prefer to develop their listening skills. In this chapter, we begin by outlining how students are oriented toward listening activities via their general learning styles. Because individual students have their own preferred learning styles, and because these styles can sometimes be predicted by factors such as ethnicity, age, type of task, and previous learning, we can often tailor our listening programs to suit the types of learners we have. Although students may have preferred learning styles, this is not to say that they cannot use other styles. To expose learners to other learning styles (which may be more effective in the task at hand), teachers can introduce their students to a range of listening strategies.

According to Willing (1988:7), a learning strategy is "a specific mental procedure for gathering, processing, associating, categorizing, rehearsing, and retrieving information or patterned skills." In this chapter, we illustrate a wide range of listening strategies that students may either already possess or can be introduced to. Students can become aware of their listening strategies either through specific learning training sessions or by the teacher's integration of strategy training into the listening lessons. We illustrate how the teacher can introduce both of these approaches.

5.2 General Learning Styles

Learning styles are the approaches students prefer to adopt when learning, and they are generally consistent behavior. Learning style is a concept that has been developed from the extensive work into cognitive styles, that is, how people think and act in certain ways. Psychologists attempted to find out how to measure intelligence and, as a result, developed instruments that illustrated how people approach learning tasks. Two main distinctions that

Table 5.1 *Description of Learning Styles*

Deep Approach	Surface Approach	Strategic Approach
Learners who put all their efforts into trying to understand something. They believe everything they learn is worthwhile.	Learners who try to gain only enough information to complete a given task.	Learners who focus on assessment and grades and learn only in order to pass a test.

Field-Independent (Holistic)	Field-Dependent (Serialist)
Learners who attempt to gain an overall understanding by focusing on general features. They often approach their learning in a personal way and relate new knowledge to existing knowledge.	Learners who try to build up their knowledge in a systematic, step-by-step way.

Converger	Diverger
Learners who believe that there is a "correct" answer or a "correct" way to do things. They develop patterns of learning and keep to these established patterns.	Learners who are creative in their thinking and approach their learning in an open-ended manner.

Concrete	Abstract
Learners who like to have examples and conceptualize their learning in terms of their own experiences.	Learners who like to generalize and rely on developing overall principles for their learning.

Reflective	Active
Learners who build up their knowledge by stopping to consider what they have learned. They deliberately think about their learning.	Learners who like to explore and experiment with their learning. They like to find their own solutions to tasks and problems.

Solitary	Social
Learners who like to learn by themselves.	Learners who like to learn with others.

The information used in this table is explained in more detail in Kyriacou et al. 1996.

emerged in cognitive styles are field-dependency and field-independency (Witkin et al. 1977). A field-dependent person likes to learn step by step in a sequential way. A field-independent person likes to learn in a holistic way, preferring to get the "big picture" rather than the details. This initial information about cognitive styles led educationists to develop other instruments, which illuminated a range of styles of preferred learning behavior. Information about the main types of learning styles is summarized in Table 5.1. As can be seen, there are several distinct types of learners. For instance, Biggs (1987), who based his work on information-processing theories (Chapter 2), determined that there were three types of learners. One type included those who were intrinsically motivated to learn and who would employ a range of strategies to gain as full an understanding as possible – *deep learners*. Then there were *surface learners*, those students who were driven by fear of failure and relied heavily on rote learning devices. The third type included those who employed strategic approaches to their learning – *strategic learners*. These learners were usually well organized and had a competitive drive to their learning.

It would be wrong, though, to assume that a surface learner could never become a strategic learner. The categories of learning styles in Table 5.1 must be considered as ranges on scales, rather than fixed styles of learning. Where students are on a scale may be affected mostly by personality, but factors such as task type, time of day, level of interest, and motivation may also affect the ways in which learners approach their learning and the style of learning they adopt. Learning styles develop through the use of different learning strategies or tactics. But although learners can be trained to use strategies and hence change their learning styles, left to their own devices they usually have preferences in how they approach their learning (Kyriacou, Benmansoure, and Low 1996).

One issue raised from the study of learning styles is what we should do with this information about our students' learning styles. If we think that students are not using the most efficient learning style, should we force them to change? Or should we instead change our teaching methods to suit the students? Some studies suggest that to create a better learning environment and encourage students to take part in their learning, teachers should change the methods they use in class to suit the learning styles of their students (see Violand-Sanchez 1995). In many of these situations, however, culture clash is as much a problem as is teaching context. Often minority students join classes where the dominant learning style is at odds with their previous learning. In order to cater to such students, teachers need to make some changes to the way classes are conducted. On the other hand, when a teacher is aware that students are not using the most efficient learning styles, the teacher needs to consider how best to introduce those learners to new styles. This is often done by encouraging the learner to develop a large repertoire of learning strategies.

Task 1

Convert the categories in Table 5.1 to points on a scale, with one scale for each set of styles. Then decide on a listening task you need to perform in your L1. Mark on the scale where you think you would be in relation to adopting particular learning styles for each listening task. Discuss your ideas with a partner. For example:

Solitary ————————————————— Social

Listen to a   Watch a movie
lecture   with a friend

Rationale: Listening to a lecture is something you need to concentrate on in an individual way. However, there may be times when you ask your neighbor a question about the lecture to check your understanding, which is more social. Going to a movie with a friend is a social activity; it is something you plan to do for fun. On the other hand, during the movie you are not likely to check your comprehension with your friend. Thus, these two situations have solitary and social aspects of learning.

One way to assist students in finding out what kind of learners they are is to administer a learning style questionnaire or quiz. Based on the extensive research into this area by Willing (1985, 1989), Nunan (1996) drew up such a questionnaire (Figure 5.1). In this questionnaire, students are required to score each of the sentences and find out which type of learner they are. Types 1 and 3 are probably learners who are more inclined to use top-down approaches in their learning, whereas types 2 and 4 indicate learners who probably use more bottom-up approaches to learning. Any combination of scores that covers more than one type possibly indicates students who like to use an interactive approach to learning. Finding out about the types of learners in a class can have implications for the syllabus or the way in which the syllabus is introduced to the learners.

Task 2
Use the learning style questionnaire (Figure 5.1) to find out what type of learner you are. Do you agree with the result? How might the results of a general descriptor such as this influence how you develop listening skills?

5.3 Learning Strategies

Choosing the "best" learning strategy is not always an easy task, given that there are hundreds of strategies students can choose from. O'Malley et al. (1985) report that, in an investigation of high school ESL students' use of strategies in integrated learning tasks, no fewer than 638 strategies

WORKSHEET - LEARNING STYLES

How do you like to learn?

For each of the following types score yourself 0, 1, 2, or 3 in the brackets to show how you like to learn best.

0 = no   1 = occasionally   2 = usually   3 = yes

Type 1

I like to learn by watching and listening to native speakers.   [   ]

I like to learn by talking to friends in English.   [   ]

At home, I like to learn by watching TV and/or videotapes in English.   [   ]

I like to learn by using English out of class.   [   ]

I like to learn English words by hearing them.   [   ]

I like to learn by having conversations.   [   ]

TOTAL [   ]

Type 2

I like the teacher to explain everything to us.   [   ]

I want to write everything in my notebook.   [   ]

I like to have my own textbook.   [   ]

In class, I like to learn by reading.   [   ]

I like to study grammar.   [   ]

I like to learn English words by seeing them.   [   ]

TOTAL [   ]

Type 3

In class, I like to learn by playing games.   [   ]

In class, I like to learn by looking at pictures, films, and videotapes.   [   ]

I like to learn English by talking in pairs.   [   ]

At home, I like to learn by using audiotapes.   [   ]

In class, I like to listen and to use audiotapes.   [   ]

I like to go out with the class and practice English.   [   ]

TOTAL [   ]

Type 4

I like to study grammar.   [   ]

At home, I like to learn by studying English books.   [   ]

I like to study English by myself (alone).   [   ]

I like the teacher to let me find my mistakes.   [   ]

I like the teacher to give us problems to work on.   [   ]

At home, I like to learn by reading newspapers.   [   ]

TOTAL   [   ]

Add up your score for each section and put a number in the *Total* box. The highest total shows what kind of learner you are.

Look at the descriptions below:

Type 1: If you have a high score in this section, you are probably a good communicator. You enjoy interacting with people and using the English you have learned in a natural way.

Type 2: If you have a high score in this section, you probably enjoy learning English in class. You like the teacher to lead you through learning the language.

Type 3: If you have a high score in this section, you probably enjoy learning English by examples. You like learning with other people and you see learning a language as fun.

Type 4: If you have a high score in this section, you probably like learning English by studying it in detail. You like to work by yourself and find out how to use the language on your own.

Figure 5.1 Learning styles questionnaire (From "What's My Style?" by D. Nunan, in *Tasks for Independent Language Learning*, edited by D. Gardner and L. Miller, 1996. Reproduced by permission of TESOL, Inc.)

were identified. This wide range of strategies, however, could be classified into 20 distinct categories, and these categories encompassed the three main areas of strategy use: metacognitive, cognitive, and socioaffective (see Brown and Palincsar 1982). *Metacognitive strategies* are the ways learners organize, monitor, and evaluate their learning. *Cognitive strategies* are the processes learners use to acquire the language. *Socioaffective strategies* are the ways in which learners use others to enhance their learning and encourage themselves to continue learning.

Oxford (1990) has been one of the most prominent researchers and writers in the field of language learning strategies. Her Strategies for Independent Language Learning (SILL) has become one of the most widely accepted tools to investigate learning styles. Oxford's SILL is composed of a six-part questionnaire of 50 statements, which learners score using a Likert scale of 1–5, 1 being "Never or almost never true of me" and 5 being "Always or almost always true of me." The six sections are divided as follows:

Part A = Remembering more effectively (memory strategies)
Part B = Using mental processes (cognitive strategies)
Part C = Compensating for missing knowledge (compensation strategies)
Part D = Organizing and evaluating learning (metacognitive strategies)
Part E = Managing emotions (affective strategies)
Part F = Learning with others (social strategies)

By completing the SILL, learners discover the type of learning strategies they most favor. This information, when made available, can then sensitize teachers to the most suitable methods for teaching specific groups and can show where students may lack certain strategies considered important for certain tasks. For instance, Littlewood (1996) found that the Asian (mostly Hong Kong Chinese) students he surveyed did not like to take responsibility for the assessment of their learning. It may therefore be assumed that these students would score low on Part D of Oxford's SILL – organizing and evaluating learning. However, a valued skill for university students is to be able to work independently of teachers and be able to know how well they have mastered a certain knowledge base without relying on formal tests. It might be appropriate, therefore, to expose Littlewood's students to some form of metacognitive learning strategies as part of their induction programs into universities so that they may be able to evaluate their own learning more effectively. Culture has been identified as one factor that affects the types of learning strategies learners favor (see Tyacke and Mendelsohn 1986; Reid 1987). Other factors can be seen in Table 5.2.

Task 3
Choose a listening activity to analyze from any textbook (or find one in Chapter 7). Look at the factors in Table 5.2 that affect use of strategies. Decide which factors would affect the activity you analyzed and what the teaching implications are. Discuss your ideas with a partner.

The implication of knowing about the strategies learners use is that teachers may be able to adapt their teaching methods to suit specific groups

Table 5.2 *Factors Affecting the Acquisition and Use of Strategies*

Factor	Description
Language to be learned	Teachers of various languages might use different teaching methods to teach their languages. This in turn will affect the type of strategies learners are exposed to or can use to learn the language.
Language level	Intermediate listeners report using more metacognitive strategies than do novice listeners (Vandergrift 1997).
Knowledge about self	Learners who have been challenged to think about themselves as language learners may be more aware of the strategies they use and do not use. Knowledge about one's personality (e.g., introvert vs. extrovert) may also affect the type of strategies learners use.
Sex	Studies have shown that women exhibit more learning strategies than men, and that men and women have preferred strategy types (Nyikos 1990).
Motivation	The more learners want to succeed in learning a language, the greater their range of strategies.
Learning style	Strategies depend on the overall style of learning (see Section 5.2).
Career orientation	Learners who are involved in pursuing careers that are language related use a greater range of strategies than other learners (Oxford 1989; Reid 1987).
Language teaching methods	Learners are influenced by the ways in which they are taught. The longer they are exposed to certain teaching methods, the more they rely on the strategies implied by those methods.
Task requirement	Different tasks require learners to utilize different strategies. For example, in a group work activity, learners will probably use more social strategies than when performing an individual writing task.

of learners, and they may consider introducing new strategies to expand learners' repertoires so that they can listen effectively in different situations.

5.4 Effective and Ineffective Listening Strategies

Research has illustrated that not all of the strategies learners use are effective in helping them listen. O'Malley and Chamot (1990) tell us that there are significant differences between effective and ineffective listeners on aspects such as checking comprehension, elaborating, and inferencing. These researchers found that "whereas the effective listeners used both top-down and bottom-up approaches, the ineffective listeners used only a bottom-up approach to comprehend" (O'Malley and Chamot 1990:132). However, the research into what is effective is still unclear because other researchers studying types of listening used in formal test situations found that L2 learners use bottom-up processing more often than they use top-down processing (Tsui and Fullilove 1998).

In an earlier study, O'Malley, Chamot, and Kupper (1989) found that effective and ineffective listeners differed in three main ways: perceptual processing, parsing, and utilization.

Perceptual processing. Effective listeners are aware of when they stop attending and try to redirect their attention to the text. Ineffective listeners are often put off by the length of the text and by the number of unknown words they encounter. When they stop attending because of these factors, they do little to redirect their attention to the text.

Parsing. Effective listeners usually attend to larger chunks (or parsing) of information and only attend to individual words when there is some message breakdown. They utilize intonation and pauses and listen for phrases or sentences. Ineffective listeners tend to focus more on a word-by-word level – a bottom-up strategy.

Utilization. Effective listeners use world knowledge, personal knowledge, and self-questioning as a way of attending to the message. Ineffective listeners use these elaboration techniques less. Whereas effective listeners can be described as actively participating in the listening process, ineffective listeners are more passive.

Although some learners may be categorized as possessing ineffective strategies, there are many examples of how these listeners can be trained to increase their strategy repertoire and use the strategies they have more effectively (Derry and Murphy 1986; O'Malley et al. 1985; Weistein and Mayer 1986). The following learner training idea is adapted from Wong (1996). The teacher needs to first prepare a worksheet similar to that shown in Figure 5.2. More examples of worksheets that help orient students toward their language learning can be found in Ellis and Sinclair (1989) and Gardner and Miller (1996).

Task 4

Prepare a listening needs analysis questionnaire for a group of learners with whom you are familiar. Consider carefully the type of learners you have in mind, and decide on the most suitable format for the questionnaire. *Hint*: Young learners will need a more user-friendly questionnaire than the one shown in Figure 5.2, whereas advanced learners may need more flexibility.

Prioritizing Your Listening Needs

Information to the Student: Below are some common situations for which you need to develop listening strategies. Decide which situations you need to develop your listening skills for—now and in the future. Do not tick too many as you cannot work on them all at the same time. It is better to choose the most important situations and focus on them. Write a number 1 to 5 to indicate how proficient you feel you need to become in that situation.

After you have prioritized your listening needs, use the table below to make a plan of action to develop your listening skills. You then have targets which you should work toward, either in class or in your own time.

Language focus: Listening	Needs		Proficiency (1 = very poor; 5 = very good)
	Now	Future	
Conversations			
Dictations			
Discussions			
Entertainment			
Instructions			
Lectures			
TV (state type of program)			
Radio (state type of program)			
Songs			
Talks and presentations			
Telephone conversations			
Others:			

Figure 5.2 Worksheet for prioritizing learners' listening needs (Adapted from "Focus on Your Language Needs" by M. C. P. Wong in *Tasks for Independent Language Learning*, edited by D. Gardner and L. Miller, 1996. Reproduced by permission of TESOL, Inc.)

5.5 Listening Strategies in the Classroom

A second way in which students can become aware of how to develop better listening habits is by the integration of listening strategies into language lessons. From a think-aloud procedure (a technique in which learners are asked to record their thoughts or strategies as they perform a language task), with learners listening to various texts in a second language, Vandergrift (1997:392–4) produced a summary of listening strategies. Figure 5.3 is based on Vandergrift's taxonomy, but in the figure, we illustrate how each strategy can be implemented in the controlled environment of the classroom.

5.6 A Strategy-Based Approach to Teaching Listening

In this section we illustrate a strategy-based approach to develop listening skills in an English for specific purposes (ESP) context. We outline stages of a listening lesson in a course specially prepared for first-year engineering students at a university in Hong Kong (see Miller 2001 for a full description of this course).

The conceptual underpinnings of the listening section of the English for Engineering course are oriented around two main foci: a task-based approach and a strategy-based approach. On entering the English-medium university in Hong Kong, the Cantonese-speaking engineering students need to be able to function with ESP in a variety of ways, one of which is to listen to engineering lectures from native and nonnative English speakers (British, American, Australian, Indian, Singaporean, and Chinese). In order to help the students meet this need, a series of target and pedagogical tasks (Long and Crookes 1992) was developed for the students' first-semester language course. The target tasks are listening to segments of authentic spoken text on an engineering topic. The pedagogical tasks are specially prepared exercises and activities that enable the learners to complete the target tasks. In preparing the preset pedagogical tasks, consideration is given to what listening skills can be developed through the texts. For example, some texts have general discussions and summaries in them. These texts are suitable for global listening. Other texts have more detailed information and specifications. These texts can be used for listening for specific information. The tasks are structured around a simple format of pre-, while-, and post-task activities to facilitate overall language learning.

The second focus of the ESP listening course is to make the learners aware of the strategies they use while completing the tasks and how they

METACOGNITIVE STRATEGIES

Planning	Focus on the Learner	Focus on the Teacher
Strategy		
● Advanced organization	Decide what the objectives of a specific listening task are. Why is it important to attend to this message?	Write a topic on the board (e.g., Train Announcements) and ask learners why it would be important to listen to this type of announcement.
● Directed attention	Learners must pay attention to the main points in a listening task to get a general understanding of what is said.	In setting up a listening task, ask learners what type of information they would expect to hear. "You are listening to the news. What would you hear at the beginning of the news?"
● Selective attention	Learners pay attention to details in the listening task.	Before listeners listen a second time to a recording, set specific types of information for them to listen for. "Listen again to the tape and find out what type of relationship the speakers have."
● Self-management	Learners must manage their own motivation for a listening task.	Before setting up a listening task, the teacher chats with the students in the L2 so that they get their mind frame around listening to the L2.
Monitoring		
● Comprehension monitoring	Checking one's understanding.	The teacher sets up a task that requires listeners to understand one part of the task at a time. They monitor in stages so that the final part is easily understood.

Figure 5.3 Listening strategies and their pedagogical implications. (Adapted from "The Comprehension Strategies of Second Language (French) Listeners: A Descriptive Study" by L.Vandergrift, 1997. Reproduced by permission of ACTFL.)

	Focus on the Learner	Focus on the Teacher
• Auditory monitoring	Learners make decisions as to whether something sounds "right" or not.	The teacher asks learners to use the L1 to determine their perception of spoken text. For example, the teacher asks learners to listen to a tape and decide how the characters feel; then students check with one another in their L1.
• Double-check monitoring	Checking one's monitoring across the task.	At the end of a task, the teacher asks learners to review their previous knowledge about the speakers and make any changes to their perception of what the message is about.
Evaluation	**Focus on the Learner**	**Focus on the Teacher**
• Performance evaluation	Learners judge how well they perform a task.	The teacher can use a variety of techniques to get students to judge their individual performance. For instance: "Raise your hand if you think that you understood 100%; 75%; 50%."
• Problem identification	Learners decide what problems still exist preventing them from completing the task successfully.	After completing a listening task, the teacher asks students to identify any part of the text that was difficult to comprehend.

Figure 5.3 (Continued)

COGNITIVE STRATEGIES

Inferencing	Focus on the Learner	Focus on the Teacher
Strategy		
• Linguistic inferencing	Guessing the meaning of unknown words by linking them to known words.	Before a listening task, the teacher writes some difficult vocabulary on the board so as to draw attention to these words. The teacher then plays the tape and asks students to listen for the new vocabulary and try to guess the meaning from their understanding of the whole text.
• Voice inferencing	Guessing by means of the tone of voice.	The teacher focuses the learners' attention not on *what* is said but on *how* it is said.
• Paralinguistic or kinesic inferencing	Guessing the meaning of unknown words by referring to paralinguistic clues.	Teacher discusses with the learners how certain features of the speakers' actions in the video can help them guess the meaning of the message.
• Extralinguistic inferencing	Guessing based on other clues, such as what is required in the task.	The teacher informs the learners that they will listen to a long stretch of speech. The teacher then writes some questions on the board to direct the learners' attention.
• Inferencing between parts	Making use of certain words in the text that may not be related to the task to get more information about the task.	The teacher points out that the information at the beginning of the text will help the learners understand the later sections of the text.

Figure 5.3

75

Elaboration	Focus on the Learner	Focus on the Teacher
• Personal elaboration	Learners use prior personal experience to comprehend the task.	At the beginning of a lesson, the teacher asks learners to talk about any experiences they have had that relate to the topic.
• World elaboration	Learners use their world knowledge to comprehend the task.	At the beginning of the lesson, the teacher activates the learners' schemata on certain topics by asking general questions about a topic.
• Academic elaboration	Learners use knowledge gained during their formal learning experiences.	During a listening task, the teacher can ask learners if they have encountered similar experiences in other disciplines, such as knowledge of countries in their geography lessons.
• Questioning elaboration	Learners question themselves about what they do know, and what they do not know about a topic.	The teacher sets up brainstorming sessions before, during, or after a listening task for learners to question themselves about what they know about the situation.
• Creative elaboration	Learners try to adapt what they hear to make the story more interesting to themselves.	The teacher has learners brainstorm different endings of a story and then listen for the real ending.
• Imagery	Learners use mental imagery to create a picture of what is happening.	The teacher asks learners to keep their eyes closed while listening to a story and try to picture what is happening.

Figure 5.3 (Continued)

76

	Focus on the Learner	Focus on the Teacher
Summarization	Learners make a mental or written summary of what they hear.	The teacher asks the learners to give an oral summary to each other, or to write one sentence to summarize what they have listened to.
Translation	Learners translate from the first language verbatim what they hear in the second language.	The teacher asks learners to talk with each other in the L1 and try to translate what they have listened to. Or, if the teacher is bilingual, the learners can translate what they heard for the teacher to check.
Transfer	Learners use knowledge about their first language to facilitate listening to the second language.	The teacher could draw student's attention to words in the L2 that are similar to words in the L1.
Repetition	Learners repeat words they listen to so that they become familiar with the sounds.	The teacher sets up a shadow listening task. In this task, the learners look at the text while listening to a story. While listening, they read the text quietly to themselves.
Resourcing	Learners use any resources to aid them in their understanding (e.g., dictionaries, diagrams, notes, peers).	When appropriate, the teacher focuses the learners' attention on artifacts that will help them understand the task. For instance, "Look at the diagram before you listen to the story."
Grouping	Learners group words together based on common attributes.	The teacher activates the learners' schemata on certain areas so that they are aware that the information they hear will have something in common with their previous knowledge.

Figure 5.3

	Focus on the Learner	Focus on the Teacher
Note taking	Learners write notes as they follow some spoken text.	The teacher assists the learners in making notes that will help them comprehend the message. These notes can be in skeleton form or free form.
Deduction/Induction	Learners apply rules they have learned or have developed themselves to follow a text.	The teacher either explains the rules of a particular part of speech or has learners guess what the rules are by listening to a text.
Substitution	Learners substitute words they know to fill in gaps in their listening to see if their overall comprehension makes sense.	The teacher asks students to give a variety of words or expressions to compensate for certain parts of the text they listen to. For instance, "The man said 'Could you close the door?' What else could he have said?"

SOCIOAFFECTIVE STRATEGIES

Strategy	Focus on the Learner	Focus on the Teacher
Questioning for clarification	Learners find out more about the text by asking questions.	The teacher gets learners to ask questions related to the task before, during, or after their listening to a text.

Figure 5.3 (Continued)

Cooperation	Learners work together to pool their comprehension.	The teacher asks learners to work in pairs or groups to discuss what they heard and find out from each other what they understand about the text.
Lowering anxiety	Learners try to relax before listening to the message.	The teacher has the learners close their eyes for one minute before beginning the listening task and asks them to think of something that makes them feel happy.
Self-encouragement	Learners develop a positive attitude toward the task and believe that it is possible for them to understand what they will hear.	The teacher asks the learners to set themselves a personal standard for the listening task. For example, "If you only understand 20% of the text, that's OK."
Taking emotional temperature	Learners realize that sometimes they will not feel happy about listening in a second language.	The teacher asks learners to keep a journal about how they feel during their listening tasks. These journals can be private, so that no one else will read them, or they may be open for the teacher and/or learners to read and comment on.

Figure 5.3

79

might develop their language-learning strategies. Exposing learners to a range of language learning strategies gives them the opportunity to find out which strategies work best for them. These language-learning strategies can then serve as the basis of future language development and, it is hoped, be used when learners listen to content subject lectures.

5.6.1 A Classroom Example

In the following example, we outline one lesson from the English for Engineering course. The video worksheets are based on *Manufacturing Technology* (Laleman and Priess 1994), a video on the development of manufacturing technology in industry. This American-produced video is aimed at high school students and is intended as an introduction to manufacturing engineering. The video is in seven segments. The topics in the video are about manufacturing technology, manufacturing systems, manufacturing resources, and manufacturing processes. Each segment lasts from seven to twelve minutes. The lesson described here comes from the middle of the course, so the students are already familiar with the video. Figure 5.4 shows the stages of the lesson, the procedure the teacher follows, and the strategy enhancement targeted.

As can be seen from the brief outline of an ESP listening lesson, the students are encouraged to use a wide range of listening strategies. Students may already be familiar with some of these strategies and may use them when they attend lectures (e.g., world elaboration or academic elaboration). Other strategies may not be so familiar to these Chinese students (e.g., lowering their anxiety level and note taking; see Flowerdew and Miller 1995). By exposing students to such a wide range of listening strategies in language lessons, we make them aware of a greater array of listening skills.

Task 6
Look at a unit from a textbook you are familiar with (or find one from Chapter 7). Make a list of the listening strategies you can promote when teaching this unit or activity (refer to Figures 5.3 and 5.4).

5.7 Conclusion

In any consideration of how best to develop effective listening skills in students, some attention must be given to how students learn, their preferred

Stage	Procedure	Strategy
1	Teacher chats with students in the L2 for several minutes about their course—how things are going, what they did in the workshop this week.	Motivational management
2	Teacher introduces the topic of the listening task, "Manufacturing Systems," and asks students to think about this for a few minutes.	Advanced organization
3	Teacher announces that he/she will play the video through once. The students should listen for the general ideas about a system within manufacturing engineering, but they should also relax and try to enjoy the video.	Directed attention Lowering anxiety
4	After some general feedback about what a manufacturing system is, the teacher announces that he/she will play the tape a second time. This time students are directed to the stages in the system. "Try to find out what the stages of the system are and listen for any part the speaker emphasizes."	Between part inferencing Stress and Intonation patterns (voice)
5	This time, the teacher asks the students to work in groups of 3 or 4 to draw up a few points about the description of the system they have been listening to.	Cooperation Performance evaluation Personal elaboration Academic elaboration World elaboration
6	Teacher distributes a skeleton handout of the video segment. Students listen once more and complete the notes.	Note taking Academic elaboration World elaboration
7	Teacher pairs up students and asks them to practice giving an oral summary of the video from the notes they prepared.	Summarization Performance evaluation

Figure 5.4 Outline of an ESP listening lesson

styles, and what strategies they employ. Although learning styles rely to some extent on personality, there are ways in which teachers can introduce their students to other styles and then allow the students to decide which method works best. One way to orient students to other learning styles is via the strategies they use when listening. The two ways in which teachers can introduce students to listening strategies are by specific learning training programs or by integrating learning skill objectives into their regular teaching programs.

5.8 Discussion

1. Look at Table 5.2, on factors affecting strategy choice. Can you think of any other factors that affect learners? What are the pedagogical implications of these other factors?

2. Vandergrift (1997) used a think-aloud procedure to discover his learners' listening strategies. Discuss other procedures that can be used to find out about learners' listening strategies. Consider the advantages or disadvantages these procedures would entail. For example, *keeping a journal*: advantage – gives learners time to reflect on their learning; disadvantage – there may be a time delay and learners will forget what strategies they used.

3. Identify a group of learners you are familiar with. What effective listening strategies do they use most often? Do they use any ineffective listening strategies? How do you know?

4. What style of learning do *you* adopt when learning a second language (see Table 5.1)? How do you know this?

5. Identify a group of learners you are familiar with. What are the main factors (see Table 5.2) that affect their use of strategies?

PART II:
A PEDAGOGICAL MODEL AND
ITS APPLICATION

The following three chapters, Chapters 6–8, form the second part of this book. We begin in Chapter 6 by presenting a new pedagogical model of listening. This model is centered around what is already known about listening, as laid out in Part I of the book. However, we maintain that existing models of the teaching of listening are narrow in focus, and we believe that a wider perspective is required. Therefore, we introduce further dimensions.

To illustrate how the pedagogical model can be used, in Chapter 7, we evaluate a selection of listening textbooks. In this chapter, we show that many of the dimensions of our model are missing from existing listening material. We do not, though, claim that every dimension of the model is required in all listening material. What we do maintain is that, through the selective introduction of aspects of the model to learners, they will be encouraged to develop more complete listening abilities.

To test the pedagogical model further, in Chapter 8, we present a series of case studies, taking the reader into contexts where the teacher is explicitly attempting to help students develop their listening skills. We see, through the case studies, that although some of the dimensions of the model may be present in some instances, there are still opportunities for further development of listening skills, based on the dimensions in our pedagogical model.

6 *A Pedagogical Model for Second Language Listening*

6.1 Introduction

The theoretical knowledge we have reviewed in Part I of this book has been applied to a greater or lesser extent over the last several decades to teach listening. Bottom-up, top-down, and interactive models of accounting for the listening process (Chapter 2) have been used extensively, as have insights concerning different types of meaning (Chapter 3). Theories of the nature of spoken language (Chapter 4) and of listening strategies (Chapter 5) have started to be applied only recently and selectively.

In this chapter, we map out what we consider to be the essential features of a pedagogical model of second language listening. Our model consists of a set of dimensions derived from those theories reviewed in Part I, along with insights from other theories. These dimensions are eclectic, insofar as they draw on cognitive, social, linguistic, and pedagogical theory. Drawn together, they can enable us to develop a unified model of second language listening.

The model we propose has at its heart the cognitive models of listening (see Chapter 2):

Bottom-up processing
Top-down processing
Interactive processing

But it also has distinct dimensions of listening that give a more complex structure. It is

Individualized	Affective
Cross-cultural	Strategic
Social	Intertextual
Contextualized	Critical

Our model does not have a distinct place for "language proficiency," as we do not consider this to be a distinctive *listening* skill, on the one hand, and

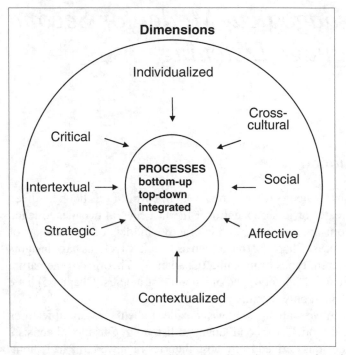

Figure 6.1 A model of second language listening comprehension

because it may be incorporated as a part of the other dimensions, on the other. The model is represented schematically in Figure 6.1.

We stress that each of these dimensions should not be applied equally in every listening course or lesson, but rather that there is potential for a consideration of each of the dimensions on the part of teachers and course developers. Ultimately, they will decide to what extent, if any, the dimensions might be focused upon. The application of the model could be as a checklist in designing a listening course or in evaluating/adapting listening materials. We emphasize again, however, that we do not expect that every dimension will be relevant or applicable for every listening course or activity. The following sections set out our new pedagogical model of second language listening.

6.2 Dimensions of Listening

6.2.1 Individual Variation

Individualized learning has been promoted at least since the 1970s (e.g., see Disick 1975) and received new impetus in the late 1980s with Nunan's

(1988) book *The Learner-Centred Curriculum*. However, to date, it has not been greatly applied to listening.

An important advantage of the interactive model over other models, whether they be bottom-up or top-down, is that it allows for the possibility of individual variation in linguistic processing (i.e., at different stages of proficiency and with different text and task types, focusing on specific types of processing is more or less appropriate). From the pedagogical point of view, this opens up the possibility of a model that is sensitive to individual learning styles, on the one hand, and the needs of particular groups, on the other. At the individual level, some people may do better using top-down processing, while others may put more emphasis on bottom-up processing. At the group level, beginners are likely to need more time developing basic bottom-up skills of decoding, whereas for learners who have mastered basic phonology and syntax, emphasis on the development of top-down skills of applying schematic knowledge may be more appropriate.

6.2.2 A Cross-Cultural Dimension

If we consider the role of schemata and background knowledge in the listening process, we encounter the question of different cultural interpretations. Different cultures are likely to give rise to different schemata and consequently different expectations and interpretations of a given (spoken or written) text. In research conducted by one of the authors, Hong Kong Chinese students were asked to provide their interpretations of a televised address by their former British governor. Their interpretations of what the governor was trying to achieve in his address were considerably different from the British researcher's interpretation. Some of the Chinese students interpreted the governor's statements in the light of Confucianist writings about government in the Chinese tradition, whereas the researcher interpreted them more in terms of the governor's British political background. Neither interpretation was wrong. Both meanings were potentially appropriate interpretations of the governor's address. It is just that the researcher and the Hong Kong students were applying different schemata and deriving different interpretations.

In this example, the cultural differences between the Hong Kong Chinese students and their British teacher were clear. There were significant differences of ethnicity, language, and nationality between the two, which gave rise to the different interpretations. But if one takes a broad definition of culture to also include gender, age, social and professional position, attitudes, values, beliefs, and general world knowledge, then we see that there is potential variation in the interpretation of a given text by any two individuals, even if they would normally be said to belong to the same culture.

The theoretical justification for the incorporation of this dimension can be found in the vast literature on cross-cultural communication that has been produced in recent years (e.g., see Scollon and Scollon 2001).

Task 1

Look at the following prelistening activity. Decide if it is appropriate to introduce cross-cultural dimensions to the activity in preparation for the listening task. For example, some students may not consider a garden to be important when renting a flat, especially students who have grown up in cities (e.g., Hong Kong Chinese) or in dry climates where gardens are not part of everyday life (e.g., Gulf Arabs).

Unit 6 Flat (Apartment) Hunting

Prelistening

1. With a partner, scan these advertisements and decide what the abbreviations mean. Make a note of them, as you will need them for the listening in exercise 3.

West St. Immac. 1st fl. 1 b. sit-rm.
New k&b gar. $95 p.w. Tel: 8342 6438

West St. Flood St. Eleg 1st fl. Maisonette
Access to gdn. 1 dbl. b. b. fitted k, c.h.
$120 p.w. Tel 8342 2748

Goodman St. Immac 2nd fl. Flat
Prize loc. Lge recet., 1 b. newly fitted
k&b, gar., no pets. $195 p.w. Tel: 8342 9260

Help Avenue. Spac. fam flat. Near sch. 2b.
quiet env. 2 bath. $220 p.w. Tel: 8324 8843

6.2.3 A Social Dimension

Bottom-up models of listening developed in the context of processing individual sounds, words, or sentences. Top-down and interactive models use more extended text. Neither type of research has considered interactive dialogue, however. While there are practical reasons for this (it is much simpler to conduct experiments using single sounds, words, sentences, or monologic texts), it is unfortunate insofar as the pervasive context in which listening occurs in the real world is dialogue. Listening, in the context of conversation, is not just a psychoperceptual process, as the models outlined in Chapter 2 might lead one to believe. It is also a very social activity, in which both speaker and hearer affect the nature of the message (see Chapter 4), on the one hand, and how it is to be interpreted, on the other. (Grice's maxims, as we saw in Chapter 3, are based on the assumption of such mutual cooperation in conversation.) Any comprehensive model of listening needs, therefore, to take conversation into account. In Chapter 4, we illustrated how recognizing the stages in a conversation – reformulation, turn-taking, and the like – were all important in listening. Although conversation may be considered as a paradigm case for the social dimension of listening, that dimension is in fact present, to a greater or lesser degree, in all types of listening, even in monologue.

Another point that needs to be taken into account regarding the social dimension of listening is the varying listener roles that may be taken up. In the paradigm case of two-way conversation, there is a listener and a speaker. In other situations, however, there may be other listeners: There may be *side participants* (people taking part in the conversation, but not being directly addressed) and *overhearers* (people listening, but not officially ratified as participants). In second language pedagogy, it is interesting to note, learners very often play the role of overhearers; they listen to recordings of conversations between other people or monologues directed at audiences other than themselves. Two things are slightly disturbing about this state of affairs. First, learners are made to adopt what is often a rather clandestine role in normal life (hence, the derogatory term *eavesdropper*). Second, because overhearers have no rights to participate and thereby guide the interaction, the learner's task is made more difficult than it would be in real life, where opportunities would be taken for staging, back-channeling, reformulating, repair, and turn-taking in order to aid comprehension.

Task 2
Choose a dialogue from a textbook. Using ideas from A Social Dimension, 6.2.3, consider how to rewrite the dialogue, incorporating a more social dimension to the listening activity.

6.2.4 A Contextualized Dimension

In our own ethnographic work on academic listening (Flowerdew and Miller 1992, 1995, 1996), one of the most striking of our findings has been the

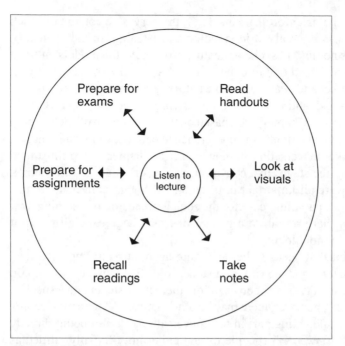

Figure 6.2 A contextualized model of listening to lectures

close integration of listening with other processes and activities. In the lecture context, students not only are required to listen to what the lecturer says but also have to read a handout and look at visual aids. They probably need to take notes. Before the lecture, they may have been expected to do some preparatory reading. And following the lecture, they may be required to participate in a tutorial and/or to do a written assignment. Later, they may have to sit for an exam. All of these activities, which accompany the listening process, are likely to affect the way an individual actually listens. One result of this multidimensional aspect of listening (see Figure 6.2) is that the meanings derived from a listening text (e.g., a lecture) may actually derive not just from that text but also from the relations between that text and other texts (spoken or written) that have been encountered or are likely to be encountered in the future.

The example we have given is of one type of listening, listening to lectures, but other types of listening are also accompanied by parallel activities. It is important, therefore, to extend the models of listening presented above to take account of these additional variables. Such an expanded *contextualized model* is particularly appropriate, we feel, where the objective is pedagogic, designed to prepare learners to listen in real-life situations, as opposed to the laboratory settings in which the earlier models were developed.

Even where the focus of listening is not constrained by additional activity and texts (e.g., radio broadcast), listeners are likely to process that text in the context of other texts. If we are listening to an item on a radio news program, for example, about the latest developments in the sex scandal surrounding a well-known personality, our interpretation of that item is likely to be affected by earlier news items that have dealt with that topic, whether on the radio, in the other mass media, or in discussion with our families, colleagues, and friends. One important ramification of this contextual view is that the way listening is traditionally taught – by means of individual texts in isolation – forces learners to listen in ways that are not natural. In not contextualizing listening in other related texts, language teachers are in fact making the comprehension process much harder than it actually is in real life.

Task 3

Look again at Figure 6.2. Draw a diagram to show how listening can be contextualized in the following: watching the news on TV; listening to a train announcement; listening to "special offer" announcements in a supermarket.

6.2.5 An Affective Dimension

Most models of listening basically try to explain comprehension. However, in this book, we are concerned with developing a pedagogical model, and we need to extend the basic models accordingly. Affective variables influence language acquisition in general, including listening, and comprehension can only take place if individuals are motivated to listen.

A pedagogical model of listening, therefore, needs an affective dimension that accounts for the decision to listen. Such a model was proposed by Mathewson (1985) for reading, although it can be easily adapted for listening.

According to Mathewson, there are four affective factors that may lead to a decision to read/listen: attitude, motivation, affect, and physical feelings. *Attitude* includes text-specific attitudes, which are determined by the content, format, or form of a text; a general positive attitude toward listening (listening is good); and the source of listening material. *Motivation* includes belongingness and love, curiosity, competence, achievement, esteem, desires to know and understand, and aesthetic appreciation. Motivation is an energizing process that is required before a positive attitude toward listening can be translated into an actual decision to listen. *Affect* refers to feelings that may contribute to a decision to listen. It includes moods, sentiment, and emotion. These feelings may vary in duration, intensity, and quality. *Physical feeling* takes account of outside sources during listening, which may affect feelings (e.g., when there is some extraneous background noise). The text itself may produce physical feelings (e.g., the feeling of pleasure from a particularly enjoyable story).

In addition to these factors, the physical presence of the speaker is an affective variable that might be added to Mathewson's (1985) taxonomy for reading. Listeners might be more (or less) inclined to listen to a real person, as opposed to an audio or video recording.

L1 models of listening assume that there is one single goal in listening: comprehension of the aural message. However, an L2 model needs to acknowledge that L2 listeners, in listening, may have another goal: a learning goal. L2 listeners want to understand the message, but they also want to develop their listening ability and indeed their overall language proficiency through listening. This goal of listening for language learning, it seems to us, is an essential dimension of an L2 model of listening, and it should be included with the other affective variables outlined by Mathewson.

Task 4

Look at any listening activity from a textbook (or choose one from Chapter 7). Which affective factors do you think it would be important to consider when teaching the activity?

6.2.6 A Strategic Dimension

An L2 model of listening needs to incorporate specific features of the second language listening process. The learning dimension of an L2 model of listening must identify the specific learning strategies that are beneficial to the acquisition of the listening skill. As we illustrated in Chapter 5, considerable research has been carried out in recent years into the ways learners use specific strategies to enhance their learning.

Traditionally in language pedagogy, as we outlined in Chapter 1, the development of listening has been seen as incidental to the learning of other knowledge and skills (most often syntax and lexis), and it has not been the focus of overt instruction. This deficiency obviously needs to be remedied. In line with recent thinking on the importance of learning strategies, language awareness, and learning to learn, this strategic dimension to a model of L2 listening must be directed toward educating learners to identify their own preferred strategies, for these strategies are likely to be most beneficial. Good language learners have *metacognitive ability*, that is, they are able to monitor their use of language consciously with a view to enhancing it. It seems to us that a model of L2 listening needs to reserve a special place for this particular metacognitive strategic dimension.

6.2.7 An Intertextual Dimension

The comparatively recent resurgence of interest in the work of the Soviet linguist Bakhtin has drawn attention to the pervasive *intertextual* nature of language: how any utterance is likely to reflect the past linguistic experience of the speaker and hearer. The contextualized view of listening we outlined in Section 6.2.4 is concerned with one type of intertextuality, in the terminology of some scholars. Here, we prefer to distinguish that broader type of textual relation, which is concerned with conceptual knowledge, from the more overtly linguistic relations that for us constitute intertextuality.

The sorts of things that we mean by intertextuality are to be found in the following examples. In a television advertisement for Thai International Airlines, a voice whispers the words *smooth as silk*. This phrase is a commonly used idiom in English, but when used in this particular context, it takes on a second meaning; smoothness does not refer to a surface here, but to the smooth ride and smooth service one has with this particular airline. In another advertisement, an international accountancy firm, Arthur Andersen, is promoted with the slogan "Business unusual." This is a play on the well-known expression "Business as usual," the change designed, no doubt, to suggest the originality of the service offered by this particular firm of accountants. In a further example, the Four Seasons hotel chain uses the slogan "Some people get all the breaks." This is a well-known expression, but here there is a play on the word *break*, which brings together two meanings, "good luck" and "short holiday."

In addition to advertisers who adapt everyday language, attaching new meanings in specific contexts, everyday conversation often draws on advertising language for its own uses. Some L2 postgraduate students were recently bewildered when their British lecturer indicated the end of the first part of a two-part lecture with the words: "Have a break. Have a Kit-Kat" – a slogan he borrowed from a popular advertising campaign for a particular brand of chocolate biscuit. Everyday conversation may also borrow from other media besides advertising. In a recent BBC World Service radio program, a well-known concert violinist characterized the British cultural identity as adventurous and innovative by borrowing an expression from the well-known *Star Trek* science fiction television program. "I think we boldly go where others haven't been before," she stated, thus adding extra force to her utterance by echoing language used by space adventurers of the future.

Intertextuality also functions at the level of *register* – how language is used by particular social groups (teachers, students, the police, airline pilots, etc.) or in particular fields of discourse (education, policing, aviation, etc.). And it functions at the level of *genre* – how language is used in particular recurrent situations to achieve particular communicative goals (service encounters, television soap operas, lectures, textbooks, etc.). Different registers and genres have their own recurrent patterns of language use, or intertextuality, which listeners need to be able to recognize. In this respect the notion of intertextuality is similar to that of schemata (Chapter 2), although the latter are concerned with more than just language.

Intertextuality is thus pervasive in all forms of language, including casual conversation. It is an aspect of comprehension that demands a high level of familiarity with the target culture over and above knowledge of the basic language system. Whatever the challenges (given its pervasiveness), a model of L2 listening needs to incorporate intertextuality at some level.

Task 5
Make a list of as many examples of the intertextual nature of language as you can think of.

6.2.8 A Critical Dimension

In considering intertextuality from the point of view of listening, we are concerned with how the spoken message we hear is related to other texts. Texts, of course, are social artifacts, produced by individuals situated within particular societies, at particular times, and in particular places. If texts are social in nature, they can be said to represent society. At the same time, however, society, to a certain extent at any rate, is made up of texts, by what people say; our conception of reality is necessarily mediated through language. If we consider texts in this way, then listening becomes a political activity, because what we hear is imbued with the assumptions, or ideologies, that are shared by the society that produced the texts.

Given the inequalities in power among members of contemporary society and the potential for exploitation of the less powerful by the more powerful, the possibility arises of a critical approach to listening, an approach that seeks to interpret language critically in light of the unequal distribution of power. As van Dijk (1997) has noted, it is the powerful who, to a large extent, control the social context in which language is used. The powerful members of society tend to control the setting, participants, topics, style, rhetorical patterning, and interaction in which discourse is created. For example, if we consider the case of Thai International Airlines and the utterance "Smooth as silk," we may realize that this utterance has a political dimension that may not strike us on first hearing. "Smooth as silk," in the context of the television advertisment, is accompanied by an image of a beautiful young female cabin crew member. It is not unreasonable to "read" this image as suggesting that it is the woman, or one of her peers, who will make travel with Thai airways "smooth." Women are thus demeaned by the utterance "smooth as silk" and its accompanying images. To take another simple example, when we buy our McDonald's hamburger, and the serving staff enjoin us to "have a nice day" or to "enjoy your meal," this is most likely not a personal wish by the staff member concerned; it is a result of the social context in which the individual finds him/herself, the fact that all McDonald's workers are required to produce this utterance every time they serve a customer.

What this might suggest for a model of listening is a critical component that encourages listeners to analyze the context in which what they hear is created and thereby deconstruct it so as to reveal the inequalities of power that the text reproduces. This may seem a demanding requirement best left to advanced students, but if we think about our examples from the airline and the fast food chain, the utterances we analyzed, from a strictly linguistic point of view at any rate – "Smooth as silk," "Have a nice day," and "Enjoy your meal" – are hardly complex. They could quite appropriately be used in teaching at the most elementary levels. The great merit of incorporating such a critical dimension into a model of listening is that it introduces a level of sophistication to language learning that is often in danger of trivialization. At the same time, of course, language teaching has the opportunity of preparing learners for responsible citizenship (Fairclough and Wodak 1997).

6.3 A Listening Dimensions Evaluation Checklist

Table 6.1 shows a checklist based on the listening dimensions discussed in this chapter. This checklist can be used to evaluate existing materials, with a view to supplementing the material, or new materials, to see if they are suitable for use with particular groups of learners.

The checklist is best used in conjunction with the overall aims and objectives of a course or with the specific aims and objectives of particular

Table 6.1 *A Checklist: Dimensions of Listening*

	Yes	No	Don't Know
Type of processing involved			
• Bottom-up			
• Top-down			
• Interactive			
Does the exercise/activity have the following dimensions?			
• Individualization			
• Cross-cultural aspects			
• Social features			
• Contextualized dimensions			
• Affective factors			
• Strategic aspects			
• Intertextuality			
• Critical discourse features			

Now look at the aims and objectives of your course/lesson. Based on the evaluation, does the exercise/activity match your aims and objectives?
Yes = use the exercise/activity
No = adapt the exercise/activity
No = discard the exercise/activity
Don't know = consult another teacher

lessons to see if any adjustments to the material are necessary. In Chapter 7, we suggest a list of questions, based on the dimensions of listening, that can be used to develop specific materials. Those questions can be used along with this checklist.

In the checklist there are three columns to tick: Yes, if the dimension exists; No, if the dimension does not exist; and Don't Know, if the evaluator is unsure. If the Don't Know box is ticked, then it is advisable to seek assistance from a colleague in evaluating the material.

Once an evaluation has been done, the evaluator must look at the aims and objectives to see if the materials suit them. If any dimension is ticked as No, a decision needs to be made as to whether the material needs this dimension to fulfill the aims and objectives of the course or the lesson.

6.4 Conclusion

Bottom-up, top-down, and interactive models of accounting for the listening process have been used extensively over the past decades to teach listening. However, we believe that they do not cater to the complexities of the listening process, a process that also encompasses individual, cultural, social, contextualized, affective, strategic, intertextual, and critical dimensions, as shown in Figure 6.1. This chapter has attempted to draw these dimensions together to show how a pedagogical model of second language listening might be conceptualized.

Task 6

Use the checklist in Table 6.1 to evaluate one textbook listening activity for a particular group of learners. Based on the results of the evaluation, would you recommend using the material as it is, adapting it, or not using it at all?

6.5 Discussion

1. Look at Table 6.1 again. Discuss how you already take account of these factors when teaching listening. If there are some factors that you do not take into account, explain why not. Specify the group of students you teach.
2. Which of the dimensions of listening outlined in this chapter would your students have the most difficulty with?
3. In this chapter, we mention a critical dimension to listening. How easy or difficult do you think it would be to introduce this to elementary language learners? How would you teach the examples given in Section 6.2.8?

7 *Materials and the Pedagogical Model for Listening*

7.1 Introduction

In this chapter, we analyze listening material from a selection of textbooks. We describe how four English language textbooks, from beginner to advanced level, help learners develop their listening skills. After the brief descriptions, we apply the model described in Chapter 6 to see how the different dimensions are accommodated in the materials. We do this by way of tables. We highlight which dimensions of the model may be present in the material and describe the types of activities we found and which language and learning skill objective may be present. It is important to note, however, that we would not expect all the dimensions mentioned in our model to be present in each unit of a textbook, and so the purpose of applying the model is not to show deficiencies but only to illustrate which dimensions of the model are present. After the textbook analysis, we offer a checklist of questions that material writers might consider using when preparing listening materials. Then we show how one piece of material, specially prepared to assist students develop their listening skills, can be supplemented to take account of the new model and the different dimensions of listening.

7.2 Beginners

7.2.1 About the Book

On Target! (Holt 1999) is an integrated language skills book for young learners – 6 to 11 years old. The introduction to the teacher's guide describes the materials as having a "building-blocks" approach to the development of language whereby content and skills are integrated. Students are encouraged to learn the language appropriate to performing certain tasks and activities, thereby making the language learning meaningful. The students' resources include a students' resources book, worksheets, monolingual (English only) cassettes and compact discs, and grammar practice books.

There are four resource books for the students to work from: Books A to D. The contents of the resource books are thematically based. The themes in Book D (highest level) are colors, noises, and the seasons; then there are two projects, *All about Me* and *Animals*. These projects can be integrated into the syllabus or can be used as stand-alone units and presented to the students after they have completed the target units.

7.2.2 About the Class

Level: Beginners
Context: EFL primary school class (large class of 40 students, monolingual context)
Time to complete one unit: Four to five lessons (30 minutes per lesson)
Projects: Two or three lessons
Class makeup: Children (10–11 years old)
Materials: Resource book, colored pens, scissors, pen, paper, straws, thread, and adhesive tape

7.2.3 Description of Lesson

PROJECT 2: MAKING AN ANIMAL MOBILE

This lesson comes after the students have had lessons on the names of various animals, which pets they have, where animals live (at home, on a farm, in a zoo), and descriptions of animals (big, small, tall, long, short). In this lesson, students must listen to instructions on how to make an animal mobile, given by the teacher in the L2.

  I. Prelistening Activity: Teacher holds up different pictures of animals and asks class to shout out the names.
 II. Demonstration: Teacher holds up a completed animal mobile and asks students whether any one of them has something like this at home. Then the teacher tells students that today they are going to make a mobile.
III. Getting Ready: Teacher distributes four pieces of paper to students and tells them to take out their pencils, colored pens, and scissors.
IV. While-listening Activity: Teacher gives the following instructions to the students. Each instruction is repeated several times. Between the instructions the teacher circulates and checks that all students are on

task. Students may receive individual help when necessary (possibly in the L1).

Instructions

a) Draw four different animals on your pieces of paper.
b) Color the animals in.
c) Cut out the animal shapes.
d) Take the two straws and stick them together in the middle with sticky tape.
e) Tie a small piece of thread to each end of the straws.
f) Fix one animal to the end of each piece of string.

V. Postlistening Activity: At the end of the lesson, the teacher asks some students to hold up their mobiles and has the rest of the class call out the names of the animals on them.

7.2.4 How the Activities Fit into the Model

Listening Dimension	Description of Activity	Language Skills Objective	Learning Skills Objective
Individualization	Learners have choices as to which animals they wish to draw.	Listen and decide which animals to draw.	*Metacognitive strategies*: • Advanced organization • Directed attention *Cognitive strategies*: • Personal elaboration • Creative elaboration
Cross-cultural aspect			
Social features	Students can chat with the teacher as s/he circulates and helps them. However, this may happen in the L1, in which case the social features of the L2 would not be practiced.	Checking instructions with teacher on an individual basis. Getting information about animal names.	*Metacognitive strategies*: • Comprehension monitoring • Double-check monitoring *Cognitive strategies*: • Inferencing between parts • Imagery • Translation *Socioaffective strategies*: • Questioning for clarification

Listening Dimension	Description of Activity	Language Skills Objective	Learning Skills Objective
Contextualized dimension	The students have a task to do and so the language is contextualized within the task.	Following instructions to complete a task.	*Metacognitive strategies:* • Directed attention • Selective attention • Auditory monitoring *Cognitive strategies:* • Linguistic inferencing • Paralinguistic inferencing • Personal elaboration • Translation
Affective factors	The postlistening activity, in which students hold up their mobiles for the rest of the class to see, may act to encourage students to do a "good job" on similar tasks in the future.	Listen and respond to encouragement/praise from teacher.	*Metacognitive strategies:* • Performance evaluation • Strategy evaluation *Cognitive strategies:* • Voice inferencing *Socioaffective strategies:* • Taking emotional temperature
Strategic aspects	Students need to develop specific listening skills in order to complete the task. Listening to instructions.	Listening to imperatives at beginning and following instructions.	*Metacognitive strategies:* • Directed attention • Selective attention • Auditory monitoring • Strategy evaluation *Cognitive strategies:* • Inferencing between parts • World elaboration • Question elaboration • Transfer • Resourcing *Socioaffective strategies:* • Self-encouragement

Listening Dimension	Description of Activity	Language Skills Objective	Learning Skills Objective
Intertextuality	Throughout the lesson, the students relate their comprehension to previous knowledge about the language of animals and about the genre of "instructions," with its use of imperatives and parallelism (i.e., words, phrases, clauses, and structures that are repeated in different contexts).	Listeners make use of previous knowledge.	*Cognitive strategies*: • Imagery • World elaboration • Personal elaboration
Critical discourse features			

Comments

In the project activities of Holt (1999), most of the dimensions in the listening model are accounted for. Those that appear to be missing are cross-cultural and critical discourse features. These, perhaps, are challenging features of the model to account for at the beginner level because young learners are less sophisticated in their self- and world perceptions. Again, we emphasize that not all the dimensions of our model would be expected to be relevant all the time.

Holt (1999) adopts a task-based approach (see Chapter 1). Students are required to *do* things with the language and must become active participants in their learning. In the sample lesson described here, students must develop a range of learning strategies in all three areas: metacognitive, cognitive, and socioaffective. The course book does a good job in making students aware of their listening skill potential.

Task 1

Choose a beginner-level textbook. By yourself or with a partner, analyze a unit of the book according to the eight dimensions, language objectives, and skill objectives. What does your analysis tell you about the book? If any of the dimensions or objectives are missing from the book, would you attempt to introduce them? How would you do this?

7.3 Low-Intermediate

7.3.1 About the Book

Trio 2 (Radley and Sharley 1999) is a revised edition of a listening/speaking book first published in 1987 by Heinemann International and the British Council for Thai secondary schools. This revised edition is updated and colorfully presented. The book has 60 lessons in ten units. Each unit has a grammar objective in a communicative framework. The book is used with Form 8 students, that is, 14- and 15-year-olds.

Although the book's focus is on the oral/aural skills, there is a secondary focus on reading and writing. Each lesson in the book follows a prescribed format with a listen-and-read section to begin with and then a series of speaking/listening activities.

7.3.2 About the Class

> Level: Low-intermediate
> Context: EFL secondary school class (large class, 40 students)
> Time to complete one unit: 50 minutes
> Class makeup: Teenagers (14–15 years old)
> Materials: Textbook, tape cassette, pen, and paper

7.3.3 Description of Lesson

UNIT 3, LESSON 4: WHAT'S HER NAME?

   I. Listen and read: Students listen to a taped recording and read a dialogue between two men talking about finding a suitable milkman to deliver milk. They talk about two possible assistants, a boy and a girl. The dialogue is tightly structured around giving personal information in reply to *Wh-* questions: What's her name? Where does she live? The listening activity lasts around three minutes.

  II. Answer: Students listen to the conversation again and complete a chart about the girl and the boy. They listen for name, age, address, hobbies, and description.

III. Listen and repeat: Students listen to the question format on the tape and repeat what they hear: What's her name? What's his name?

IV. Write and speak: Students are directed to look at the dialogue in Activity I and find all the questions. They need to write the questions in their notebooks. Then they practice asking each other the questions and giving the appropriate reply for the boy and the girl in the textbook.

V. Write and speak: Students copy a chart similar to that in Activity II. They fill in the chart with information about themselves first; then they interview a partner and fill in his/her information.

VI. Listen: Students listen to a new conversation about a film producer looking for a boy and a girl to act in a new movie. The producer has a conversation (similar to that in Activity I) to find out information about two possible candidates. Students listen only and complete a personal information form.

VII. Write: Students are given a cloze passage about the girl the producer in Activity VI was enquiring about. Then they write a similar paragraph about the boy.

7.3.4 How the Activities Fit into the Model

Listening Dimension	Description of Activity	Language Skills Objective	Learning Skills Objective
Individualization	Activity V. Write and speak. Students use their personal information to complete the chart.	Using *Wh*- questions to ask for personal information	*Metacognitive strategies:* • self-management *Cognitive strategies*: • personal elaboration • transfer • note taking *Socioaffective strategies*: • cooperation • self-encouragement
Cross-cultural aspect			
Social features			

Listening Dimension	Description of Activity	Language Skills Objective	Learning Skills Objective
Contextualized dimension	Activities II, V, and VI. Note taking.	Listening for specific information	*Metacognitive strategies:* • directed attention • selective attention *Cognitive strategies:* • summarization • note taking *Socioaffective strategies:* • cooperation • questioning for clarification
Affective factors			
Strategic aspects	Activity I. Listen and read.	Identifying the sound/symbol relationship in English words	*Metacognitive strategies:* • auditory monitoring • directed attention *Cognitive strategies:* • imagery • resourcing
	Activity III. Listen and repeat.	Mimicking the correct intonation and stress in *Wh*-questions	*Metacognitive strategies:* • performance evaluation *Cognitive strategies:* • repetition
Intertextuality			
Critical discourse features			

Comment

In *Trio 2*, students seem to be exposed to a limited range of listening dimensions, namely, individualized, contextualized, and strategic dimensions. Although we illustrate only one lesson here, the remainder of the units in the book follow a similar format, so that few of the other dimensions are catered for. In this unit, there may be a cross-cultural dimension to the material if the teacher exploits the concept of "milkman." Milkmen are not common in Thailand, and students will not be familiar with the concept. However, the material is designed for Thai English teachers, and these teachers need to be familiar with the cultural context of the material in order to introduce this dimension. The material itself does not help the students understand the concept.

Trio 2 claims to use a communicative approach, but the listening activities have more in common with grammar, discrete-item, and audio-lingual approaches. Because of the approach taken in this book, the material has a limited range of listening dimensions, and teachers would need to supplement the textbook heavily in order for students to develop their listening skills fully.

Task 2

Choose a low-intermediate level textbook. By yourself, or with a partner, analyze the book according to the eight pedagogical dimensions, language objectives, and skill objectives. What does your analysis tell you about the book? If any of the dimensions or objectives are missing from the book, would you attempt to introduce them? How would you do this?

7.4 Intermediate

7.4.1 About the Book

Great Ideas (Jones and Kimbrough 1997) is a listening/speaking course book used in a private language school in Rio de Janeiro, Brazil. The book provides the syllabus for an oral/aural fluency course. This course may be taken as a stand-alone course or in conjunction with another course aimed at developing intermediate reading or writing skills. Students attend 1 hour 45 minute classes once a week for 10 weeks. Therefore, the teacher must select the unit on which to focus from among the 15 units. The units need not be done in sequence. And indeed, the activities in each unit do not always follow a sequence (see description of lesson in Section 7.4.3), so the teacher may choose certain activities for the students to try and ignore other activities if it is felt that they are not suitable, or if there is not enough class time.

In the teacher's introduction we are told that each unit of the book is based around a pre-, while-, and postlistening format. The units are task-oriented, and the focus is on having students perform realistic communicative activities. As such, there are no comprehension questions because we rarely need to answer such questions in real life. The authors of the book have developed the tasks so that students are required to gather and share information.

7.4.2 About the Class

Level: Intermediate
Context: EFL private language school (class size around 20 students)
Time to complete one unit: 1 hour 45 minutes
Class makeup: Mixed adults (16–50 years old)
Materials: Textbook, tape cassette, pen, and paper

7.4.3 Description of Lesson

UNIT 2: STRANGER THAN FICTION

I. Listening: Students listen to a tape recording about two Italians. While they listen, they need to note all the coincidences about the two men. They then work in pairs to compare their notes and talk about the coincidences.

II. Communicative activity: Students work in pairs, one reading information about Abraham Lincoln, the other about John F. Kennedy. Then they share the information and try to find out what was similar about these two men.

III. Identical twins: All students read a short story about identical twins and then work with a partner to identify all the coincidences in the twins' lives. Then students must walk around the class talking to as many other students as possible to try to find a "partner" who has things in common with them.

IV. True or False? Students are presented with some information about a famous psychic. They then have small-group discussions around three questions:

1. Do you believe in ESP?
2. Have you ever heard about ESP incidents?
3. Have you ever had an ESP sensation?

V. Superstition: Students work with a partner to write out a list of superstitions. They then work in small groups to discuss superstition.

VI. Communication activity: Students use some guided questions to interview each other about horoscopes, lucky/unlucky numbers, wishes, and the like.

VII. Is it all in the mind? Students work in small groups to discuss such phenomena as ghosts, the Bermuda Triangle, and UFOs.

VIII. A picture is worth a thousand words: Students look at four unusual photographs in the book and work with a partner to make up a story about what led up to the picture. (For example, a lady is standing in the middle of her kitchen. She is surrounded by earth and has a spade in her hand.)

7.4.4 How the Activities Fit into the Model

Listening Dimension	Description of Activity	Language Skills Objective	Learning Skills Objective
Individualization	Activity III. Find a partner	Use of expressions like • Do you like . . . ? • What day were you born? to elicit personal answers.	*Metacognitive strategies*: • selective attention • auditory monitoring *Cognitive strategies*: • questioning elaboration • personal elaboration
	Activity IV. True or false	Questions help students talk about their beliefs/feelings.	*Socioaffective strategies*: • cooperation • questioning for clarification *Metacognitive strategies*: • self-management • performance evaluation *Cognitive strategies*: • linguistic inferencing • voice inferencing • world elaboration
	Activity VII. Is it all in the mind?	Students give opinions.	*Socioaffective strategies*: • cooperation *Metacognitive strategies*: • self-management • performance evaluation *Cognitive strategies*: • linguistic inferencing • voice inferencing • world elaboration *Socioaffective strategies*: • cooperation

Listening Dimension	Description of Activity	Language Skills Objective	Learning Skills Objective
Cross-cultural aspect	Activity V. Superstitions	Students make statements about superstitions in their own culture.	*Metacognitive strategies*: • advanced organization *Cognitive strategies*: • personal elaboration • world elaboration *Socioaffective strategies*: • cooperation
Social features	All activities	Students work in pairs or small groups to discuss issues.	*Metacognitive strategies*: • directed attention • selective attention *Cognitive strategies*: • personal elaboration • world elaboration • translation *Socioaffective strategies*: • cooperation
Contextualized dimension	Activity I. Listening activity	Students listen for main points.	*Metacognitive strategies*: • directed attention • selective attention *Cognitive strategies*: • summarization • note taking
Affective factors	All activities	Students are constantly required to listen to their partners and monitor what they say.	*Metacognitive strategies*: • advanced organization • directed attention • self-management *Cognitive strategies*: • questioning elaboration *Socioaffective strategies*: • cooperation • lowering anxiety • self-encouragement • taking emotional temperature

Listening Dimension	Description of Activity	Language Skills Objective	Learning Skills Objective
Strategic aspects	Activity I. Listening activity	Note taking	*Metacognitive strategies*: • directed attention • selective attention *Cognitive strategies*: • summarization • note taking
	All other activities	Students listen for details of personal opinions/information.	*Metacognitive strategies*: • directed attention • selective attention *Cognitive strategies*: • personal elaboration • questioning elaboration *Socioaffective strategies*: • cooperation
Intertextuality			
Critical discourse features			

Comments

Nearly all the dimensions of the listening model are accounted for in *Great Ideas*. This book has both a communicative and a task-based approach. A large amount of individualization is inherent in the activities, as students are allowed to choose the ways in which they listen and then decide what to do with the information they have. Because the book is aimed at fluency practice, most activities rely on students adopting a top-down approach. It is somewhat surprising that such a sophisticated holistic approach does not cater to intertextuality or critical discourse features.

Task 3

Choose an intermediate-level textbook that includes listening activities. By yourself or with a partner, analyze the book according to the eight dimensions, language objectives, and skill objectives. What does your analysis tell you about the book? If any of the dimensions or objectives are missing from the book, would you attempt to introduce them? How would you do this?

7.5 Advanced

7.5.1 About the Book

Contemporary Topics: Advanced Listening Comprehension (Beglar and Murray 1993) is a textbook specifically aimed at students preparing to attend university lectures. There are 12 units in the book, each accompanied by a taped lecture. Each unit deals with a different topic (e.g., comics, advertising, computers, memory). Review tests are printed at the back of the book along with answer keys for the tests and unit exercises. Finally, there are specially prepared lecture transcripts at the end of the book for each "lecture." The transcripts have been sanitized and are not presented in their original form (i.e., they do not contain the original hesitations, fillers, backtracking, etc.; see Chapter 4). The lectures are approximately 1,500 words long and last for around 12 minutes. The lectures are given by a variety of speakers.

7.5.2 About the Class

Level: Advanced
Context: College ESL students (in U.S.A.)
Time to complete one unit: 2 hours 30 mins (spread over two lessons)
Class make-up: Young adults (18–22 years old)
Materials: Textbook, tape-cassette, pen, and paper

7.5.3 Description of Lesson

UNIT 4: MEMORY: OUR KEY TO LEARNING

I. Topic preview: This short two-paragraph text introduces the topic of the unit. Students read this independently and perhaps before the lesson.

II. Warm-up questions: There are four warm-up discussion questions, which are meant to stimulate the students to talk about the topic and their own personal experiences of memory in general.

III. Vocabulary preview: The vocabulary review section is divided into two parts. First, there are 12 multiple-choice statements with the "new" vocabulary boldfaced and italicized. Students must match the new word with the most similar word or expression listed below. The second vocabulary section is a list of 33 words and expressions that are in the lecture the students listen to. These are divided into two groups, "Terms from Psychology" and "Terms from Psychology Experiments." Students are instructed to read the lists and discuss any words or expressions they do not know.

IV. First listening: During the first playing of the lecture, students are asked to listen for the main ideas. The lecture is broken down into four parts. For each part, there are two multiple-choice statements or questions.

V. Second listening: During the second playing of the tape, students are asked to listen for details and facts. This time, while they listen, they must tick as true or false a series of statements. Once more, these statements are matched with the four parts of the lecture.

VI. Note-taking practice: Students are reminded of the three main points of the lecture – that there are three types of memory, three ways of measuring memory, and three ways of improving memory. They are then asked to listen once more to the tape and make their own notes under the heading of the three main points.

VII. Reviewing the content: This section points out a feature of lectures, which is that during a lecture the speaker will often use examples. Several ways of introducing examples are given: *Here's a good example of this.* . . . Students are then asked to review their notes taken from the lecture and in pairs give examples from their own experience or from what they heard on the tape about six terms (e.g., short-term memory).

VIII. Taking the test: Students are instructed to look over their notes and the vocabulary lists in this unit in preparation for the test during the next lesson. In the next lesson, the tape of the lecture "Memory: Our Key to Learning" is played once. Then students turn to the back of their textbooks, where there are four questions based on the information on the tape. Students are not allowed to use their notes while taking the test.

IX. Project: In preparation for the project, students are instructed to find a reading related to the topic of the lecture they listened to and report the reading to members of their class. In addition to this task, they are asked to read a short text (420 words) about how to learn vocabulary and then discuss the techniques in the article and their personal experiences of using techniques to learn vocabulary.

7.5.4 How the Activities Fit into the Model

Listening Dimension	Description of Activity	Language Skills Objective	Learning Skills Objective
Individualization	Project	Extensive speaking and listening; integration of any vocabulary learned in the first lesson	*Metacognitive strategies*: • double-check monitoring *Cognitive strategies*: • personal elaboration • world elaboration • academic elaboration *Socioaffective strategies*: • cooperation • self-encouragement
Cross-cultural aspect			
Social features			
Contextualized dimension	Note-taking practice	Listening for main points	*Metacognitive strategies*: • directed attention • selective attention *Cognitive strategies*: • summarization • note taking
Affective factors	Topic preview warm-up questions	Reading and thinking about the topic	*Metacognitive strategies*: • advanced organization • directed attention *Cognitive strategies*: • personal elaboration • questioning elaboration *Socioaffective strategies*: • questioning for clarification • cooperation

Listening Dimension	Description of Activity	Language Skills Objective	Learning Skills Objective
Strategic aspects	Listening to the lecture	Listening for main points; then listening for details	*Metacognitive strategies:* • directed attention • selective attention *Cognitive strategies:* • linguistic inferencing • voice inferencing • academic elaboration • imagery • resourcing
Intertextuality			
Critical discourse features			

Comments

As has already been seen, the dimensions that are integrated into the activities the students have to do in the unit are individualization, contextualization, affective factors, and strategic aspects. However, the tasks and exercises in the unit do not cover the cross-cultural aspects, social features, intertextuality, and critical discourse features of listening. This may not appear as surprising, given that students are being prepared for a transactional type of listening whereby they need to absorb information and possibly transfer this into notes. However, college students need to be trained not only in transferring spoken text into written notes but also in making judgments about what they hear, how this information fits into their already developed scheme of knowledge, and what, if any, are the cultural implications. This type of critical listening may be more important in social sciences than in hard sciences, but students do need to differentiate, for example, between core information and when the lecturer is making personal comments.

The material presented in this book is lively and intended to motivate students to want to listen. The approaches used rely heavily on an integrated approach and a strategy approach – although the strategies are somewhat limited to an academic environment.

Task 4

Choose an advanced-level textbook. By yourself or with a partner, analyze the book according to the eight dimensions, language objectives, and skill objectives. What does your analysis tell you about the book? If any of the dimensions or objectives are missing from the book, would you attempt to introduce them? How would you do this?

7.6 Preparing and Piloting Listening Comprehension Materials

Many teachers rely on the type of published materials exemplified earlier, and many of the published materials on the market do a very good job in helping learners develop listening skills. However, teachers may need to supplement textbooks when they believe that there is an obvious gap, or they may prefer to develop their own specially produced materials to cater to the specific needs of their learners. In this final section, we offer a checklist of questions, based on the model we have presented. When supplementing textbooks or developing new materials, teachers are encouraged to consider the following questions and see to what extent the materials cover the various aspects of the model.

GENERAL

- Do the materials encourage learners to focus on developing bottom-up listening skills (e.g., sounds, intonation, word stress) or top-down listening skills? Or do the materials aim to cover both areas?

INDIVIDUAL VARIATION

- How do the materials help learners individualize their learning?
- Do some groups of learners have similar needs/wants? How can the materials cater to a variety of needs/wants?
- Are the materials suitable for only one level of learner, or can they be used with a variety of levels?

CROSS-CULTURAL DIMENSION

- Are any cultural aspects of languages emphasized in the materials? (Examples might be the different ways in which similar expressions are used across cultures: "Good morning; how are you?" "Where are you going?" "Have you eaten?" which are all ways of greeting in different cultures.)
- Are there any obvious cultural difficulties learners might have with the materials?

SOCIAL DIMENSION

- How much of the material is centered on dialogues?
- How are learners generally expected to use this type of material (e.g., develop overall comprehension skills or focus on such aspects of dialogues as openings, closings, back-channeling, and turn-taking)?
- In the dialogue, are learners required to take on different roles? How is this done?
- Are the listening materials integrated with speaking materials? To what extent does this happen? Are there any problems with integrating the listening and speaking materials?
- Does the dialogue conform to natural spoken language or is it more like written text?

CONTEXTUALIZED DIMENSION

- Are the listening materials contextualized with other processes or activities?

  Listen – take notes
  Listen – read
  Listen – follow graphics

AFFECTIVE DIMENSION

- Is anything built into the materials that will affect the learners' motivation (e.g., getting them in the mood for listening, indicating how important a particular listening skill is, accounting for physical feelings)?

STRATEGIC DIMENSION

- Do the materials help learners develop specific listening strategies?

  Metacognitive – planning their learning (instruction as to what to do before a particular listening activity)
  Cognitive – while they are learning (help in doing the tasks)
  Socioaffective – after they have learned (reflections, self or with a peer, after the task is finished)

INTERTEXTUAL DIMENSION

- Do the texts of the materials relate to texts or features of texts learners have previously encountered? Should aspects of the texts that relate to other texts be drawn to the attention of the learners?

CRITICAL DIMENSION

- Do the materials cover any sociopolitical dimensions of the language (e.g., the language of power/domination)?
- Are learners encouraged to analyze the language they listen to critically?

7.7 An Example of Specially Prepared Listening Material

In this section we examine one piece of material that was developed to improve listening skills. This material was prepared for use as self-study. However, we illustrate here how it can also be used in class with a group of students. The material is taken from *Tasks for Independent Language Learning* (Gardner and Miller 1996: 83–4)

Listen and Match is an activity that helps learners tune in to different varieties of spoken English. First, the material developer records a selection in which English speakers of different nationalities talk about themselves. This tape is then either made available to the learners or used in class. The students can use a simple worksheet in four parts:

Part 1. Learners listen to the tape and record the number of speakers, male and female, talking about themselves.

Part 2. Learners listen again to the tape and try to guess the nationality of each speaker.

Part 3. Listeners try to find some distinguishing features of the speakers' speech. That is, they try to describe how they know a speaker is American, Australian, British, and so on.

Part 4. Learners are encouraged to choose the accent they most like listening to and try to imitate it. Or, as a class, students may attempt to mimic the various accents and see which one they find easiest to copy.

7.7.1 Limitations to the Material

There are two problems with this material: the unevenness of level of tasks and the potentially limited student benefits from the amount of time the tutor has invested in preparing the material. The preceding four tasks, which accompany the tape recording, allow the learner to work at two levels. Parts 1 and 2 are low-level listening skills and are simply recognition activities. These activities are suitable for beginners. Parts 3 and 4 are higher order listening exercises that require the learners to analyze and imitate accents.

These activities may be more suitable for intermediate-level learners. There-fore, the activities are uneven. Beginning language learners may be discour-aged from attempting Parts 3 and 4, and higher-level learners may be put off by the tasks in Parts 1 and 2.

The amount of time it may take the tutor to find and record a suitable group of speakers and then prepare a transcription for Part 3 may be exces-sive for the prescribed activities. Therefore, to maximize this effort and to accommodate the dimensions of the model we have suggested, a variety of activities can be developed from the same taped material.

7.7.2 Preparing Listening Material Using the New Model

The following activities are based on a recording of three people – a Canadian, an Australian, and a British person – having a conversation about their best and worst journeys. (The recording a teacher makes, though, could contain any combination of nationality – e.g., a Singaporean, an Indian, and a Thai speaker – or of distinct accent groups – e.g., some-one from the East Coast, someone from the West Coast, and a speaker from a southern state in America.) The context of our taped conversation is a group interview for a job in the travel industry, where each candidate must talk about his or her experiences and efforts to deal with difficult circum-stances. During the discussion, which is unscripted, the speakers talk to the interviewer and each other about their experiences. This taped conversation contains most of the features of a conversation as described in Chapter 4 – the speakers took both long turns and short turns, gave personal informa-tion about themselves, used their voices for emphasis, used some idiomatic expressions, and expressed surprise at some of the things said to them. Such rich oral text, therefore, lends itself to exploitation with our model.

Activity 1
Individualized Dimension
General Discussion with Students
How do you practice pronouncing new words?
Possible answers might be:

- Listen carefully to a tape recording and then imitate.
- Look at the transcription in a dictionary.
- Listen to the pronunciation on an electronic dictionary.
- Ask a friend.
- Ask a teacher.

Class Survey

How closely do you like your pronunciation of a new word to mimic that of a native pronunciation?

- Exactly the same.
- Quite close.
- Good enough to be understood.
- Good enough for me to be happy with.
- I don't care.

Group Discussion

Generally, which type of accent do you like listening to most, and why?

| American | English | Scottish | Singaporean |
| Australian | Canadian | Indian | Any other |

Comment

In this first task, the teacher tries to sensitize the students to the fact that there are many accents and tries to reinforce the idea that the students may prefer listening to some accents more than others. This preference will affect the way the students develop their own accents in English. This can be developed later into a "critical" dimension, when the question of how accent relates to class, prejudice, and the notion of World Englishes is discussed.

Activity 2

Cross-Cultural Dimension

Do You Agree?

Consider the following questions based on the tape:

1. Did all the speakers give the same type of personal information about themselves?
2. Would you give similar types of information if you were talking to a group of strangers?
3. Is there any personal information you would not wish strangers to know about at an interview?

Comment

This task attempts to deal with some cultural issues about what is permissible to ask strangers. The students may be asked to first reflect on what they would be willing to tell a stranger about themselves. Then either the teacher could conduct an open class discussion or the students can talk about the questions in groups. The focus here is on having the learners understand that although it may be rude in their own culture to ask some types of questions, it may not be considered rude in another cultural context, and vice versa.

Activity 3
Social Dimension
Listen and Analyze

Listen to the three speakers having a conversation and try to answer the following questions:

1. How do the speakers open the conversation?
2. What expressions are used to keep the conversation going?
3. What expressions are used to change the topic?
4. What style of talking with each other do the speakers use, formal or informal? How do you know?

Comment

Activity 3 requires learners to use a higher order listening skill. They need to listen carefully to the conversation and identify specific functions of language. The teacher may then expand this activity and ask students to think of other expressions the speakers could have used.

Activity 4
Contextualized Dimension
Listen and Write

You are the interviewer; as you listen to the tape, make some notes on each of the candidates. You may want to write down things you would like to ask more questions about later.

Comment

This activity has students contextualize their writing with what is said on the tape. The teacher may give the students a skeleton outline of the main points and ask them to complete the notes, or the students may be asked to make their own notes.

Activity 5
Affective Dimension
How Do You Feel?
Look at the following questions and discuss them with your partner(s).

1. What do you think about the way American, British, and Canadian speakers speak in English?
2. Which speaker's accent do you like most? Why?
3. If you spoke like one of the speakers on the tape, what would your friends think?

Comment

In Activity 5, students are asked to use the tape as the basis for a discussion about accents. In this way, the learners may be more interested in listening not to the content of the tape, but to the way things are said. Students' anxiety levels may be lowered as a result of not having to focus on the message.

Activity 6
Strategic Dimension
Listening Strategies
Sometimes the speakers on the tape express themselves by the *way* they say something. Their voices go up or down. Listen to the tape and try to write an example from each speaker when he/she uses his/her voice in a special way.

Expressions   Possible Meaning

1. Really
2. China
3. You haven't, have you?

Comment

This activity offers students the opportunity to practice one listening strategy – voice (see Chapter 5). From the large selection of listening strategies presented in Chapter 5, several activities could be prepared, each helping students focus on a particular listening strategy.

Activity 7
Intertextual Dimension
It Isn't What It Seems

Listen to the tape. It will be stopped at certain expressions. What is the meaning of the expression? Do you recognize it from other contexts? If so, what were these contexts?

Expression   Meaning

1. Raining cats and dogs
2. I had two minds about coming
3. I was on my last legs
4. Was over the moon

In what other situations do you think you might use these expressions to talk about yourself?

Comment

This task has students focus on idiomatic or unusual expressions and try to see if they can guess the meaning of the expressions. They need to transfer their knowledge of the expression and where they have heard it before to complete the activity successfully.

Activity 8
Critical Dimension
Do You Agree?

Listen to the first part of the tape only. Then, with a partner or in a small group, discuss the following questions:

1. Do you find that each of the interviewees has an equal say in the interview?
2. How does the language use, and the way each speaker speaks, affect your perception of him/her?
3. The interviewer begins by saying, "Ladies first." How does the lady react to this statement? Do you think she is correct to react this way?
4. Graham says that you need to be careful when traveling in China, as there are a lot of poor people. Do you think his implication that poor people equals danger is correct?
5. The interviewees say that women have less freedom to travel independently. Is this so in your country? What do you think of women traveling by themselves?

Comment

This last task focuses on the critical aspect of listening. The learners are asked to analyze critically both what is said and how it is said.

Task 5

Use the tapescript in the appendix in Chapter 4 (Section 4.6) to prepare some listening activities for a group of students you know. Explain why the activities you develop are suitable for the group of students you identify.

7.8 Conclusion

In this chapter, we have analyzed four textbooks that help students develop their listening skills. In our analyses, we applied the eight dimensions of the new model for listening outlined in Chapter 6. By doing this, we illustrated that although the books analyzed are successful in some areas of listening skill development, teachers and students using these books may need to supplement the activities in the books. We end the chapter by suggesting a list of questions that teachers might apply to their materials in deciding whether all the listening dimensions are fully catered to in the materials they use. We then show how the model can be used in the actual preparation of listening activities for use in class.

7.9 Discussion

1. In the analyses of the four textbooks in this chapter, we have identified what we believe are the skill objectives in terms of metacognitive, cognitive, and socioaffective strategies. Do you agree with our analyses? What other strategies might be practiced through the activities as they are described?

2. Few of the textbooks we analyze in this chapter appear to have intertextual dimensions. Why do you think this is so? What are some intertextual activities that might accompany the four activities in the textbooks used in this chapter?

3. In the textbooks that you analyzed in Tasks 1–4 in this chapter, what approaches to language learning do the books use? How are they reflected in the activities? What implications does this have for the application of the eight dimensions?

4. Look at a listening activity from a textbook you are familiar with. Discuss ways in which the activity can be expanded using the eight dimensions in the new model.

8 Case Studies and Their Relation to the Pedagogical Model

8.1 Introduction

In this chapter, we examine five situations in which the main focus of the course or context is developing listening skills. We present these case studies as a way of reflecting on some of the issues that have been raised in this book. In addition, we apply our model for listening presented in Chapter 6 and examine how the dimensions of the model are developed or not in each case study. As with the examination of textbooks in Chapter 7, our intention here is again not to expose deficiencies in any of the cases we examine. Instead, we intend to investigate what happens in real contexts where listening is taught or learned and, where appropriate, suggest how our proposed model might exploit the materials further.

Each of the case studies is very different, and so we attempt to set the scene first by way of a short introduction to the setting. This frames the context in which listening is developed. Then we briefly describe the courses and illustrate these with sample materials. Because of space limitations, we can use only examples of the materials, but we believe that these are helpful in illustrating what happens in each context.

After the description of each case, we apply our model. First, we look at the case and determine which dimensions of the model are applied in it. Usually, the materials themselves exploit a particular dimension. In some circumstances, however, through our personal contact with each case, we show how the teachers promote certain dimensions. Then we list those dimensions of the model that are not explicit in the materials and that teachers do not obviously exploit. Our purpose here is to show how the dimensions of the model can better account for what kind, or quality, of learning is taking place in the activity.

We provide some discussion questions at the end of each case study. These ask the reader to consider the context in which listening is presented, and we encourage the reader to reflect on whether our interpretation of the situation is correct. In our lives as teachers, many of us are too busy to examine fully what we do in class or to evaluate fully all the materials we use. We hope that after reading this book and examining these case studies, readers will be encouraged to conduct their own case studies of their teaching situations and seek out ways to help their students develop more effective and efficient listening skills.

8.2 Case Study 1 – Young Learners

8.2.1 The Setting

The setting for this first case study is a small primary school in Hong Kong, a predominantly Chinese community with a recent colonial past. As such, English has a strong presence in the community and is a much sought-after language skill for most of the local population. A good command of English gives access to higher education, the civil service, and the international job market and bestows a certain level of perceived sophistication on the user. Although English has high status in the community, it also has an ambiguous position with regard to whether it is a second or a foreign language, given that 97 percent of the population speak one common dialect of Chinese (Cantonese) and so do not need English to communicate among themselves. For some segments of the population (the middle class), English is a second language (ESL), while for others (below middle class), English is a foreign language (EFL). The distinction is in the amount of exposure each group has to the language and the needs they have for it.

Kai Chi Primary School is a small village school situated in the New Territories of Hong Kong close to the border with mainland China. The school has about 170 students, nine full-time teachers, one head teacher, and one secretary. The school consists of eight classrooms, one small office for the head teacher, a reception area, and a staff room. There is a large concrete playground and a garden where students grow flowers and vegetables for project work.

The school has a large percentage of immigrant children (from mainland China), and so it approaches the teaching of these children in a somewhat different fashion from the mainstream primary schools. In particular, the pupils from the mainland will have had little or no exposure to English in school in China, and although many of the schools in Hong Kong teach through the medium of Cantonese, English is still a prerequisite to gaining promotion into secondary school. The teaching of English therefore becomes an important element in the primary school pupils' curriculum. The pupils receive five 30-minutes periods of English per week. The teacher follows a textbook (Holt's *On Target!* 1999 – see Chapter 7). In a mainstream primary school, the teacher may be able to follow the textbook exclusively and at the pacing recommended in the syllabus. In Kai Chi Primary School, teachers make extra efforts to pace the lessons at a suitable level for the pupils, and they provide supplementary materials to give the pupils extra practice.

8.2.2 Description of the Course

Listening is usually integrated into the English lessons at the school. The teacher of Primary 5 (pupils are around 9 years old) considers that it is a somewhat arduous task to focus the pupils' attention solely on one skill for even a single period. Therefore, to provide variety in the lesson, and to ensure that students' motivation is maintained, the teacher takes the teaching point for one lesson and exploits it in a number of ways. This ensures that the language is constantly recycled.

A SAMPLE UNIT

Stage 1. The teacher reminds pupils of the previous day's lesson and asks them to spend a few minutes looking at the unit in their textbooks. Pupils silently read over the vocabulary from the previous lesson and ask their classmates how some of the words are pronounced.

Stage 2. The teacher asks pupils to look at their textbook and read the two-line dialogue. Then a game ensues. Each pupil is on a team in the class. Whenever the teacher asks for answers to questions, or for pupils to read aloud, students can gain points for their team by volunteering. As soon as the teacher asks for two pupils to read the minidialogue, a number of hands shoot up. The teacher calls on pairs of pupils to go to the front of the class and read the minidialogue.

Q: How long does it take you to go to the (name of a place)?
A: It takes me about . . . minutes to get there.

At the end of each minidialogue, the teacher praises the pupils and awards their group points.

Stage 3. Stage 2 is a lead-in to Stage 3. The teacher begins to ask pupils how they get to school and how long it takes to get to school. This leads into the listening activity.

Stage 4. Students are asked to open their books to page 27 and to look at a matching exercise. While they listen to the dialogue on the tape, they are asked to draw lines from the speaker to the time. The teacher then checks the answers with the class and praises them for getting the answers correct. Then students are asked to listen again to the tape and write words in the second activity:

Q: What does Mei Mei see on her way to school?
A: She sees the fish market.

Once more after listening to the tape, the pupils' answers are checked by the teacher.

Stage 5. At the end of the listening activity, the pupils are told to take a rest. This is a familiar part of each lesson, as all the pupils immediately put their heads on their desks and take a short rest.

Stage 6. Game. The teacher asks pupils to look at his lips and guess what he says. He then "mouths" various words or numbers, and pupils try to guess the word (e.g., *minibus, pineapple, twenty-four*). All the vocabulary is taken from the previous few lessons, and soon pupils are turning back a page or two in their textbooks to look at words after the teacher has mimed them. Correct guesses are awarded points for the group.

Stage 7. The teacher hands out a supplementary worksheet of vocabulary words. This vocabulary is not in the textbook but is considered essential for the pupils to become familiar with. The pupils are taken through the ten words and shown how to pronounce them. The teacher uses the L1 to explain what some of the words mean. All the vocabulary words in this worksheet deal with food. Therefore, as a homework exercise, the pupils are asked to draw pictures of the foods next to the words for them.

8.2.3 Dimensions of the Model Covered in the Case Study

CROSS-CULTURAL DIMENSION

One of the interesting factors in this case study is that the immigrant pupils are learning English to learn about another Chinese culture, that of Hong Kong. The textbook the pupils use has been specially written for pupils in Hong Kong and uses Chinese names and familiar places around Hong Kong as material for each unit. There is no mention of American, British, Australian, or any other L1 English-speaking context.

The pupils are introduced to a variety of places and aspects of the society in Hong Kong through English. For example, if the lesson is about "What did you do last Saturday?" then the teacher first has to introduce some of the places in Hong Kong where people go to spend their leisure. The immigrant pupils may never have been to these places, and so the teacher must first explain where they are and what happens there.

CONTEXTUAL DIMENSION

Many of the activities in the pupils' textbooks require matching up pictures to what they hear on a tape, ticking boxes, or writing one-word answers. They become used to this "listen-and-do" type of activity.

AFFECTIVE DIMENSION

A lot of the teacher's time is spent encouraging the pupils to take part in the lessons and trying, via games or team points, to maintain the pupils' motivation and interest. These aspects of the lesson are not built into the material, but they do become an integral part of each lesson because of the situation. Without the teacher skills in monitoring and encouraging the pupils, the lessons would become dull and boring.

STRATEGIC DIMENSION

The strategic dimensions observed in this case study of young learners are mostly at the level of listen and repeat, or listen and remember. The pupils are encouraged to focus on the form, sentence structure (how to ask a question) or vocabulary, rather than on the message or what to do with the message. This type of strategy is somewhat familiar to Chinese learners, as it encourages rote learning, a strategy that Chinese language learning encourages.

8.2.4 Dimensions of the Model That Appear to Be Missing from the Case Study

INDIVIDUALIZATION

There is no individualization built into the materials the pupils use. However, the teachers working at Kai Chi Primary School point out that the immigrant pupils are very hardworking and often do extra work outside of class. This may be prompted by their parents or by a desire to catch up with other classmates.

SOCIAL DIMENSION

As can be seen from the question-and-answer examples in Stages 2 and 4, the dialogues the pupils listen to and repeat are scripted and focus exclusively on form. As such, there is little or no exposure to the social dimensions outlined in Chapter 7.

INTERTEXTUAL DIMENSION

Although it is possible, in a limited way, to introduce an intertextual dimension with beginners, there is no such dimension present with the young learners in this case study.

CRITICAL DIMENSION

Because young learners may not be able to express themselves in a second language in a sophisticated way, it may not be surprising that there is no critical dimension in the material presented to the young learners. However, if the teacher uses the L1, there may be more opportunities to introduce a critical dimension to the lesson.

8.2.5 Discussion

1. Do you teach young learners? Discuss the types of pupils you work with and how you help them develop their listening skills.
2. The situation in Hong Kong is considered unusual, as the pupils learn about the local culture (which is Chinese) through English. How do you deal with cross-cultural issues with young learners?
3. Look at the dimensions of the model that *are* present in this case study. Do you agree with our analysis? What are other ways in which the types of materials presented here help students develop their listening?
4. Look at the dimensions of the model that *are not* present in this case study. Discuss how you might introduce these dimensions into the teaching material.

8.3 Case Study 2 – Using Technology to Improve Listening

8.3.1 The Setting

The setting for this second case study is once again Hong Kong. Over the past 30 years or so, Hong Kong has changed from relying on manufacturing to being a financial and service center. In the near future it hopes to become a cybercity. Technology plays a major role in the daily lives of the population. Although the distribution of wealth is not even, and most of the population belong to the low socioeconomic strata, the majority of homes in Hong Kong have a plethora of technical devices, and the region has one of the highest uses of personal computers in the world. Therefore, it is a perfect environment for helping learners learn via technology. Even the youngest student is familiar with computer games, and on starting school most students belong to the third-generation of technology users – that is, they expect to do some, or a lot, of their learning via technology.

8.3.2 The Case Study

In this case study, we illustrate how listening skills can be developed via the media in a structured and highly motivating fashion. The example we talk about began as a simple locally produced radio soap opera for young adult learners. It was a project sponsored by the Hong Kong Language Education Fund, the Quality Education Fund, and the Universities Grants Commission as a way of encouraging students to develop a positive attitude toward the use of English in the community and as a link between secondary school students and university students. Once on the air, the program became very popular among the local students, and the author was invited to supplement the program via other mediums so that students could not only develop their listening skills but also integrate them with other language skills: reading, writing, and Internet chatting.

Songbirds, written by a local Hong Kong–based academic and playwright, Dino Mahoney, was first broadcast on January 1, 1999. The program is an ongoing story about a group of characters who have much in common with the local student listeners. Each episode of the program is about aspects of students' lives (e.g., friendship, dating, lessons, exams, families, teachers, rivalry, tricks, cheating, fashion, hopes, fears, current events, secrets). All the actors are local students and teachers. But, although these actors are local, they represent a variety of accents both local (Hong Kong Chinese) and foreign (Indian, American, Australian, etc.), as is found in the community at large. The program focuses on creating close bonds among the actors, the story lines, and the listeners.

The programs are broadcast twice a week, on Saturday and Sunday, with repeats on Tuesday and Thursday evenings. The episode broadcast on Saturday (and Tuesday) is about secondary school students, whereas the broadcast on Sunday (and Thursday), is about university students. *Songbirds* is an out-of-class learning activity and relies on the students' motivation to listen. Because it focuses on students' lives and interests, the program very quickly gained a good following. In response to the success of the radio program, the author began to produce articles about the programs, with a focus on the story line and language used in the drama episodes (see Figure 8.1). These articles are written in English and published in English and Chinese newspapers in Hong Kong each week, a day

Coming *Songbirds* Episodes

Saturday's *Songbirds* is called "Daisy Wants Revenge." Daisy is furious that Emily told the Headmistress that she locked Li Bin in the storeroom. Daisy is a violent girl. Who knows what she might do to poor Emily.

Sunday's *Songbirds* is called "Computer Romance." May continues to flirt with Bill on the ICQ, not knowing that Bill is also flirting on the ICQ with Mei Li. Max also decides to chat on the ICQ. He calls himself Romeo, and he finds a Juliet, but he doesn't know what to say to her. Richard helps him find the words, and Juliet becomes interested. Meanwhile, Rosa wages her one-person battle against the wasteful use of plastic. This time she demonstrates against newspapers being sold in plastic bags.

1. Flirting on the ICQ

Flirting means to act in a playful, talkative way with someone you are attracted to. You flirt with people who you would like to date. In Sunday's *Songbirds* there are lots of examples of flirting on the ICQ. ICQ is a way of chatting directly with strangers and friends on the computer. This chatting can take place in "chat rooms." Sometimes people like to flirt with each other in the chat rooms. They do not know what the other person looks like, so they flirt with words, not with eyes or body language.

Bill, in London, is flirting with two girls at the same time, May in Hong Kong, and Mei Li in Vancouver. Below is an example of how he flirts on the ICQ with Mei Li. When people use ICQ they have to type their message quickly, as the person at the other end is waiting and may get bored. To type quickly, ICQ users often use abbreviations. See if you can understand the abbreviations used below.

Mei Li: Hi, Bill . . . r u there? . . . it's me . . . Mei Li . . . . from Vancouver.

Bill: Hi, Mei Li. How r things in Vancouver?

Mei Li: Cold . . . it's snowing.

Bill: Want me to keep you warm?

Mei Li: Yes, please, Bill.

Bill: Here, let me put my arms around you.

Mei Li: Like a brother?

Bill: Is that what you want me to be? A brother?

Mei Li: Maybe.

Bill: Only maybe?

Mei Li: Yes, Bill.

Did you understand the abbreviations? *r u* simply means "are you?" and *How r things?* means "How are things?" So we can see that a solitary *r* stands for the commonly used present form of the verb *to be*. Don't, however, try using these abbreviations in your exams. You may find that you lose a lot of marks!

Figure 8.1 An example of the kind of information given about *Songbirds* in the local press

or two before the episode of the program is aired. In this way, teachers can exploit the material in class, or students can read it for self-study.

Listening to *Songbirds* has also encouraged students' own attempts at creative writing. At the end of 2000, a radio drama script-writing competition was organized. More than 200 scripts were sent in from secondary and university students. Fifteen of those were selected for full professional production by the radio station, Radio Television Hong Kong (RTHK) and broadcast in the first three months of 2001. In this competition, students followed these guidelines (advertising information about the *Songbird's* writing competition):

- Write an eight-page drama script in English (about 15 minutes in duration) with a maximum of five characters (girls or boys or both), preferably based on existing *Songbirds* characters, but not compulsory.
- The story line should be about an aspect of student life.
- The drama scripts can be funny or serious or both.
- There should be two to five separate scenes.
- Entries may be submitted by one to ten writers, plus a collaborating teacher.

At the end of 1999, *Songbirds* went online. Listeners can now access the program or copies of the scripts via the World Wide Web. The two sites are *www.RTHK.org.hk*, for the audio files, and *www.songbirds.com.hk*, for the scripts. Students can now download the script and read it as they listen to an episode of the program. Figure 8.2 is an example of the type of scripts that are aired. The program, although scripted, aims at helping learners develop extended natural conversational skills with such features as colloquialisms, repetitions, blurred words, misunderstandings, intertextual interpretations, inferencing, and identifying accents. Basically, the features of spoken texts that are usually not covered in school textbooks. By looking at Figure 8.2, it may appear that these natural features of speech are not achieved. However, the rehearsals and acting abilities of the actors ensure that the text comes to life.

Although a teacher created the concept for the program, ideas of how the story line should progress are constantly being suggested by the listeners via e-mail messages to the author or the actors. Often the author will incorporate students' ideas into future scripts. For instance, after a story about boy triad groups (gangs) in schools, the author received e-mail messages from schoolgirls telling him that girl gangs were also a feature of school life in Hong Kong. They told him stories that they probably would not tell their teachers or parents. As a result of this information, some episodes

Songbirds: September 2000
Crouching Tigers, Hidden Dragons (follows Vampire Story)
Cast: Miss So, Alysha, Li Bin, Ted, Tony, Daisy, Anita, Iris, Synopsis

In the first scene, Tony tries very hard to get Anita to go out on a date with him again. In the second part, Miss So conducts a history lesson. She tries to use films as a way of reconstructing the past.

Scene1

Tony: Anita.
Anita: Oh hi Tony.
Tony: How are things?
Anita: Fine.
Tony: Good.
　　　(Pause)
Tony: Um . . . . Anita.
Anita: Yes Tony?
Tony: Do you think . . . . do you think we could . . . . try going out on another date together?
Anita: Do you want to?
Tony: Yes, yes I do. How about you?
Anita: Not sure. Maybe.
Tony: So that's not a 'no'
Anita: And it's not a 'yes' either, it's just a maybe.
Tony: Maybe we could go to the cinema together? See a film.
Anita: Just the two of us?
Tony: Why . . . would you rather go with some other people?
Anita: Not necessarily.
Tony: How about to-night Anita.
Anita: Tonight?
Tony: Yes.
Anita: Mmm, we could do.
Tony: Is that a 'yes'?
Anita: I haven't got any money.
Tony: I'll pay.
Anita: What about dinner?
Tony: We could go to Bendyburgers.
Anita: Bendyburgers?! Again?! Bendyburgers is boring, Boringburgers.
Tony: Okay, so, where would you rather go?
Anita: I dunno . . . what about that Sushi place, you know Sushi Wushi, where the sushi go round and round and you have to pick whichever ones you want?
Tony: Okay . . . we can go there.
Anita: Really?
Tony: Sure.
Anita: IF we go.
Tony: Right.
Anita: And, um . . . . IF we went out on this date . . . . what film would we see?
Tony: Um, I thought we could go and see Crouching Tiger Hidden Dragon.
Anita: Hmmmm.
Tony: Have you seen it?
Anita: No.
Tony: Do you want to see it?
Anita: Mmm . . . maybe.
Tony: So that's not 'a no'
Anita: No, but it's not a 'yes' either.
Tony: Okay . . . so . . . . . IF we went out on a date tonight we'd go to Sushi Wushi first and then to Crouching Tiger Hidden Dragon.
Anita: No.
Tony: (Disappointed) Oh.
Anita: We'd go to the film first and the sushi bar second.
Tony: (Happy) Okay!
Anita: IF we were to go.
Tony: (Disappointed) Right.
　　　Brief music

Figure 8.2 Excerpt from *Songbirds*, a radio drama for ESL secondary school students

about girl gangs and how to deal with that problem were introduced into the program later on.

In addition to the e-mail messages to the author and actors from listeners, the Web sites now offer chat rooms where listeners can discuss issues raised in different episodes of the program. The following is an example of how some students responded to the implication that one of the characters might be gay:

Posted by Alvin on 10/02/00 – 17:48:03
                    Message Body
I really pity Richard, who has been such a nice and helpful guy to all, but can hardly express his true feelings in front of others. While everyone can cry, rant, rave and give vent to his or her feelings in an uninhibited manner, Richard seems to be quite a lonely guy with none bothering to enquire how he feels (save that single effort by Siu Ping long ago). It's quite heart-breaking to hear that poignant outburst towards the end of the telephone conversation between Adam and Richard on the 1 Oct episode.

Posted by Anna on 10/03/00 – 15:50:53
                    Message Body
I do think that it is time for Richard to come out. He's been hiding his emotions for Adam for ages. Although he might have the risk of being resented by Adam, or evening losing a friend. I just hope that Adam won't react too strongly that will hurt Richard.

Songbirds is an illustration of what can be done via technology to encourage active listening by ESL learners (see Chapter 9). As we show, the program is highly motivating and uses both low technology (radio) and high technology (computers) to involve the listeners in the programs. Students in secondary schools in Hong Kong still practice their listening in school in a teacher-led structured format, but now, with the addition of a radio program written especially for them that tries to create believable situations with the conventions of natural speech, students' involvement in developing their listening skills has increased dramatically.

8.3.3 Applying the Model to the Context and Materials

INDIVIDUALIZATION

Obviously, individualization plays a major role in *Songbirds*. Students must listen to the program at home, and they can approach their listening in a variety of ways: Some may lie on their beds and enjoy the story, others may follow the information sheet from the local newspaper, others may choose to record the program and listen again later, and some may access the audio files and listen on their computers.

CROSS-CULTURAL DIMENSION

The scripts for *Songbirds* deal with many cross-cultural issues of relevance to Hong Kong students: plagiarism, dating practices, study habits, and so on. Although Hong Kong is promoted as an international city, many school students have little or no direct contact with foreigners. By way of the *Songbirds* scripts, these students' awareness of other cultural values is raised. For example, one of the characters is an Indian girl, and other characters, including Australian, Canadian, and British exchange students, have studied abroad. In this way, these characters discuss issues in light of their overseas experiences.

SOCIAL DIMENSION

The author of *Songbirds* tries hard to create realistic dialogues. Although the language is written down, many elements of spoken text are introduced, as is illustrated in Figure 8.2.

CONTEXTUAL DIMENSION

The contextual dimensions of *Songbirds* come into play when the programs are coupled with the students' reading of newspaper articles, their entering writing competitions, and their use of the Internet to communicate with the author, actors, and other listeners. Obviously, students need to follow and comprehend the stories to be able to take part in these other language activities.

AFFECTIVE DIMENSION

Some students display strong emotions toward the characters and story lines in *Songbirds*. This results in a high level of motivation to continue listening to the radio program each week. As it is a weekend program and repeated on Tuesdays and Thursdays at 7 P.M., the motivation for listening to the program comes from the students. This motivation is enhanced because of the topical issues raised and because the scripts are written at a level that the average student can follow.

STRATEGIC DIMENSION

Students can use *Songbirds* for both intensive and extensive listening practice. The newspaper articles allow students to focus on parts of the text that may cause problems for them, whereas the believable story lines allow for listening pleasure. Teachers can exploit the radio program in class and set up specific listening tasks for their students, and students can listen on their own volition and decide on the individual listening strategies they want to develop.

INTERTEXTUAL DIMENSION

In the example highlighted in Figure 8.1, we can see how an element of intertextuality is explored. In the newspaper information sheet, the author points out how, when "chatting" on the Internet, people tend to use shorthand forms like *r* and *u* to represent *are* and *you*. This cannot be created via radio, but during the program the students can be aware that when they hear the typing of a message the writer is most probably using these shorthand expressions.

CRITICAL DIMENSION

The author of *Songbirds* is careful not to push his own political views, but at the same time he does not avoid sensitive issues. There are many examples in *Songbirds* of critical dimensions of language. The example cited, in which a group of girls informed the author that there were girl gangs in schools and that he should include them also when talking about bullying, is a case in point.

8.3.4 Discussion

1. *Songbirds* is an out-of-class learning activity. Discuss ways in which this case study can be more fully exploited in class.
2. Do you encourage your students to listen to the radio in the L2? How do you prepare them for this? What type of programs do you suggest they listen to?

3. *Songbirds* acts as a conduit for integrating other language skills such as reading and writing. How could you integrate speaking activities with the radio program?
4. Look at the dimensions of the model that are developed in this case study. Do you agree with our analysis? What are some other ways in which the types of materials presented here help students develop their academic listening?

8.4 Case Study 3 – Academic Listening

8.4.1 The Setting

The setting for this case study is a new university in the Sultanate of Oman in the Middle East. English is used extensively throughout the Middle East primarily because of the reliance on a large expatriate workforce. In Oman, it is not unusual to find a variety of nationalities working side by side with Omanis in most medium to large-scale companies, the common language among these varied workers being English. In addition to the professional workforce, there is a reliance on workers from India employed as construction workers, waiters, maids, and the like. Once again, these workers use English to communicate with their Omani employers. Therefore, the local population perceives a ready need to be able to function at some level in English.

Although the medium of instruction at primary and secondary schools is Arabic, English is the medium of instruction at Sultan Qaboos University (SQU) in Oman. Because of the change of medium of instruction from secondary school to university, there is a mismatch between the level of students' academic English entering the university and the level required of them in their English-medium studies. On entering the university, most students are not fully prepared for English-medium study. In their first year, this means that they are unable to fully comprehend lectures given in English, for example, something that they have never had to do before. Other language skills are also lacking, but the focus of this case study is on how the Language Centre at the university went about helping students listen to lectures in English. This was accomplished primarily by providing beginning science students with an academic listening course based on a set of minilectures prepared by the Language Centre. The course was developed for students in the scientific disciplines because humanities students mainly study in Arabic.

8.4.2 Description of the Course

The coordinator for this course (one of the authors of this book) obtained the assistance of eight content subject lecturers in recording a series of minilectures on topics related to their discipline. The lectures are simple enough that they do not require a lot of specialist knowledge to comprehend. After securing the agreement of the content lecturer to make a recording, lecturers were asked to come to the video studio and speak for a maximum of 15 minutes on their chosen topic. They were asked to make their talk not too specific so that it might be of interest to a general audience as well as their intended group of students. To ensure that their speech corresponded as far as possible with natural lecture discourse, the lecturers were asked not to read from a prepared text but to speak from notes. They were also encouraged to use visual aids where possible so as to provide some contextualization. The following are the topics of the eight videos used in the class:

- Laboratory Glassware
- The Skeletal System
- The Periodic Table
- The Sand Dollar
- Proof by Contradiction
- Structure of the Leaf
- The Solar System
- Molecular Models

AIMS AND OBJECTIVES

General Aims. The general aim is to develop in the students the ability to comprehend, record, and apply the information presented in short lecture style monologues of between 3 and 14 minutes duration, on topics of general scientific interest.

Objectives. In relation to spoken texts comparable to those mentioned under "General Aims," students will be able to demonstrate the ability to do the following:

1. Understand the overall information structure – introduction, conclusion, main points, and the like.
2. Understand the speaker's purpose as it develops during the talk (e.g., introducing a topic, concluding a topic, giving an example, making an analogy, defining, describing a process, classifying).
3. Complete outline notes based on the lectures.
4. Reconstitute notes into speech and writing.

EXERCISE TYPES

Although the course was designed by the coordinator, a team of teachers worked on the materials for each lecture. The teachers were provided with a template for designing the exercise types to accompany each lecture.

STAGE 1

Guidance is provided in the teacher's notes for this stage. It takes the form of prelistening activities designed to activate or develop background knowledge, or schematic knowledge, a factor important in facilitating comprehension. These activities may focus on key concepts, key vocabulary, discourse organization, and so on. Techniques adopted can include elicitation by the teacher, discussion, group work, and pair work. In some units, an accompanying text or diagram is presented to get students talking about the topic.

STAGE 2

Stage 2 is an open-ended, learner-centered stage. Similar to Stage 1, Stage 2 is dealt with by the teacher and is not written into the students' material. Thus it requires that the teachers be well prepared to handle problems as they arise in this stage. With experience, teachers are more able to handle this approach. The rationale here is to give the students an opportunity to apply and develop whatever listening and note-taking strategies they may already have as they listen for the first time, before getting on to the formal teacher-generated exercises. Once the students have attempted this activity, they are encouraged to express any difficulties they had in following the talk. From this feedback, the teacher then has students discuss what strategies they might use to overcome their problems. For instance, students may say that they could not hear everything because the lecturer was talking too fast. The tutor can then explain to students that most learners think that lecturers speak too fast and that perhaps they need not worry too much about this. They should instead try to maintain some focus on the overall meaning of what is being said rather than try to understand everything. Other areas of discussion include these:

1. Understanding content
   - Too much new vocabulary
   - Difficult concept
   - Overall information structure of the talk unknown
   - Speaker's purpose unclear
   - Difficult sentence structures

2. Note taking
   - Cannot keep up with the speaker
   - Do not know what to write and what to leave out
   - Do not have necessary note-taking techniques
3. Note reformulation
   - Poor knowledge of sentence structure
   - Poor knowledge of cohesive devices
   - Inability to paraphrase
   - Inability to understand own notes
   - Poor knowledge of vocabulary

STAGE 3

Stage 3 is incorporated in the students' materials. It consists of a battery of exercises designed to develop certain aspects of listening ability in a systematic way.

1. Global comprehension – finding the main ideas or key concepts of the talk, breaking the talk down into sections.
2. Recognizing the speaker's purposes – students listen and try to recognize expressions indicating when the speaker is, for example, introducing a topic, concluding a topic, giving an example, or making an analogy.
3. Note taking – completing global or detailed notes on the whole or part of the talk.
4. Note reformulation – using notes to create a spoken or written paraphrase or summary of the whole or part of the talk.

8.4.3 A Sample Unit

THE ECHINODERMS (PHYLUM *ECHINODERMATA*)

This phylum consists of about 5,000 species, all of which live in salt water. Their most conspicuous characteristics are their spiny skin and their radial symmetry. An interesting feature, also, is their water vascular system. Sea water is taken into a system of canals and is used to extend the many tube feet. These latter structures have suckers on their tips and aid the animal in attaching itself to solid surfaces. Other features are the absence of any structure recognizable as a head, the absence of a brain, poor sense organs, and the presence of calcareous skeletal plates.

Figure 8.3 Text students read through before listening to the lecture

THE TEXT AND SUPPORTING WRITTEN TEXT AND DIAGRAM

We will now look at a sample unit of material to see how these aims and objectives are put into practice. The minilecture that has been selected is the

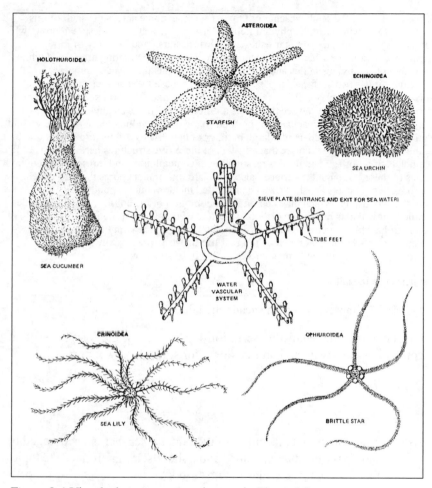

Figure 8.4 Visuals that accompany the text in Figure 8.3

shortest in the series, lasting only 3 minutes. The topic is the sand dollar, a type of echinoderm found in Oman. Before viewing the video, students are presented with a text (Figure 8.3) and accompanying visuals (Figure 8.4) to give them some useful background knowledge and to arouse their interest.

Figure 8.5 is the transcription of the talk on *Enchinodermata*. Although this lecture is very short, the information it contains is dense. On a first listening, students might be expected to get only the general idea: that the speaker is describing the structure of the animal he is holding and that there are a number of sections to the lecture (i.e., introduction, description of upper surface, description of lower surface, conclusion). This information could be elicited after a first listening. If students say they have difficulty

If we walk along the sandy beaches of Oman / we may come across the shell of this animal / it's a member of the phylum Echinodermata / which is a widespread group which includes the sea urchins / the star fishes / the brittle stars / and a variety of forms / all of them have a structure which is characterized by having five radiating arms / and whilst they are not so obvious in this animal / it nevertheless has this basic symmetrical structure / it has two surfaces / it has the hard shell / these two surfaces / the upper surface here / as we may call it / is the aboral surface / and the lower surface is the oral surface / first of all / we can see that it has a mouth here / it has an anus here / it has a number of grooves which actually bring food to the mouth / along the surface here / and you can see that it's made up of a large number of hard plates / if we turn it over and look at the other surface / we can see that you've got these five structures here / which are like the petals of a flower / and for this reason are called petaloids / and it respires through the edges of these / through the surface / also there are four minute pores through which reproductive products are shed / which are called the dermopores / and finally we see here these two slits / which may help in the locomotion of the animal / which are called lunules / now that is briefly the external structure of this / in real life it has a covering of hairs / of hair like structures / of spines / and so forth / which with time / have been washed off this particular animal / so in real life the structure is really rather more elaborate / and complicated / than we see in this dead specimen.

/ = pauses in the talk

Figure 8.5 Transcription of the academic talk

understanding the detailed description of the animal, the relevant section could be played again and broken down for students to work on.

8.4.4 The Lesson

STAGE 1

As a warm-up activity to listening to the talk, the teacher is encouraged to use the short passage, diagram, and sand dollar itself to introduce the topic. Some of the following activities may be used:

1. Ask students if they have seen any of these animals before.
2. Explain that they belong to the same phylum.
3. Ask students to describe some of the shapes in the diagram.
4. Set up a few comprehension questions on the passage to focus reading.

STAGE 2

Key vocabulary. The teacher writes the following key vocabulary words on the board and asks students to explain them or try to guess what they each mean.

symmetrical	shell	groove	plate
respire	surface	reproductive	petal
locomotion	pore	slit	spine

STAGE 3

Global Comprehension. Listen to the lecture and decide which would be the most suitable title:

1. Seashells of Oman
2. Starfish, Sea Urchins, and Brittle Stars of Oman
3. Structure of the Sand Dollar
4. Structure of Members of Phylum *Echinodermata*

Look at the following list of topics mentioned in the lecture. They are not in the same order as in the lecture. Listen to the lecture again and put the topics in the order in which they occur in the lecture.

1. Definition of phylum echinodermata
2. Description of oral surface
3. Description of aboral surface
4. Introductory statement
5. Presentation of sand dollar as an example
6. Characteristics of members of phylum *Echinodermata*
7. Structure of sand dollar in real life

Recognition of the Speaker's Purpose. Listen again to the lecture and try to recognize what expressions the speaker uses to do the following:

Points	Expressions
to introduce a specimen to his audience	*If we walk along the sandy beaches of Oman, we may come across the shell of this animal.*
to give some examples of the phylum *Echinodermata*	
to indicate that all members of phylum *Echinodermata* have certain structural features	
to indicate that his specimen is not a *particularly* good example	
to indicate that he is going to talk about the oral surface first	
to indicate that he is going to talk about the other surface	
to indicate that the lunules are the last feature he is going to talk about	
to indicate that he has finished talking about the external structure	
to conclude his lecture	

Note Taking. Listen again to the beginning of the lecture and complete the following table of notes:

MEMBERS OF PHYLUM *ECHINODERMATA*

   1. sand dollar
   2. _____
   3. _____

Now listen to the next part of the lecture and complete the notes about the external structure of the members of the phylum *Echinodermata*:

STRUCTURE OF MEMBERS OF PHYLUM *ECHINODERMATA*

Two surfaces
      Upper (aboral)
    _____

          Oral surface
             _____

             anus
             grooves – bring food to _____
             large number of _____
        _____

             5 petaloids
             _____

             4 dermopores
             _____

              shed _____
             2 lunules
              slits
              help in _____
In real life covered in _____
more elaborate

Note Reformulation: *Speaking*. With a partner, use your notes to give a short talk about the echinoderms. You can tape-record your talk and listen to it again afterwards. If you are not happy with your performance, you can re-record the talk.

Note Reformulation: *Writing*. Use your notes to write a 200-word essay on the echinoderms. Ask a partner to read your essay and make comments on it.

8.4.5 Dimensions of the Model Covered in the Case Study

INDIVIDUALIZATION

Individualization comes in Stage 2 of the typology, the learner-centered phase, where students are encouraged to apply their own strategies as they listen and to analyze the individual difficulties they may have.

SOCIAL DIMENSION

Because lectures are traditionally in the form of monologue, one might not expect there to be much, if any, social interaction going on. However, as the section "Recognizing the Speaker's Purpose" indicates, the lecturer is constantly indicating to his audience how they should interpret the direction his lecture is taking.

CONTEXTUAL DIMENSION

There are two aspects of contextualization in this example material. First, there is the skilled way in which the lecturer contextualizes his topic by introducing a specimen probably already familiar to the students. Second, there is contextualization in the supporting material. This occurs with the use of the text and diagram as prelistening material in order to develop background knowledge and with the note-taking and reformulation phase, which is a feature of the exercise typology for all of the units in the course. Of course, it should be borne in mind that each of the minilectures in the series is unrelated to the others. This is an artificial situation, because lectures will occur in a series. Being linked one to the other, of course, helps in contextualization. For this reason, some language teachers would advocate a theme-based series of lectures.

AFFECTIVE DIMENSION

As with contextualization, the affective dimension in this material is provided by the lecturer in his choice of a local example to arouse students' interest.

STRATEGIC DIMENSION

The strategic dimension of this listening course is incorporated in Stage 2, where learners are encouraged to adopt their own strategies for listening before starting on the teacher-centered exercises. This gives the students a chance to develop their metacognitive strategies, the conscious monitoring of their listening with a view to enhancing it. In the particular unit of material exemplified here, specific strategies in the teacher-centered stage focus on recognizing the discourse structure of the lecture, recognizing the speaker's purpose, and taking notes.

8.4.6 Dimensions of the Model That Appear to Be Missing in the Case Study

CROSS-CULTURAL DIMENSION

There does not appear to be a cross-cultural dimension to this material. It could be argued that because this is a science lecture and science is a universal subject, one would not expect any cultural elements to be important. However, what is interesting here is that the lecturer himself, in selecting a local species of animal to exemplify his topic, seems to be culturally aware. In our own research into cross-cultural lectures (Flowerdew and Miller 1995, 1996), we have noted how a common problem for students is that expatriate lecturers do not use local examples; instead, they use examples from their own countries that students are not familiar with. This is a point that could be made in this unit – to prepare students to deal with lectures that contain alien examples.

Another cultural issue here, perhaps, is the informal way that the lecturer introduces his topic – "If we walk along the sandy beaches of Oman, we may come across the shell of this animal." This is a positive strategy because it brings the lecturer closer to his audience. On the other hand, such an informal style may not be familiar to the students. Again, this could be pointed out.

INTERTEXTUAL DIMENSION

When one becomes familiar with the language of biology, one realizes that, certainly at the elementary level, the discipline is basically about describing structure and function. Most elementary biology texts contain many examples of these structures; thus, it can be claimed that at this level we have intertextuality. To put it another way, these types of description, or genres, use quite formulaic language, and there is thus intertextuality present.

Typical linguistic forms for describing structure, for example, are the verbs *be* and *have*, as in the following sentences from the lecture:
Be:
It's a member of the phylum *Echinodermata.*
They are not so obvious.
The upper surface is the aboral surface.
The lower surface is the oral surface.
That is briefly the external structure.
Have:
All of them have a structure.
It nevertheless has this basic symmetrical structure.
It has two surfaces.
It has the hard shell.
It has a mouth here.
These structures were not overtly dealt with in the material exemplified here.

CRITICAL DIMENSION

There is no apparent critical dimension in this minilecture. Does this mean that there is no place for a critical approach in science-based courses? Not at all. In other lectures, it would be perfectly appropriate to discuss some of the environmental and ethical issues that are important in science. Indeed, in this particular lecture, it would be possible to discuss the effect of tourism on Oman's coast and marine animals, such as the sand dollar.

8.4.7 Discussion

1. Do you teach, or have you been a student in, an academic listening course? Talk about the course and your experiences of teaching/studying it.
2. Look at the list of possible problems that students might have while listening to a lecture. What advice would you give students to deal with these problems?
3. Look at the dimensions of the model that *are* developed in the case study. Do you agree with our analysis? What are some other ways in which the types of materials presented here help students develop their academic listening?
4. Look at the dimensions of the model that *are not* developed in this case study. Discuss how you might introduce these dimensions into the teaching material.

8.5 Case Study 4 – Self-Access Language Learning

8.5.1 The Setting

The Bell School is a nonprofit educational foundation that is responsible for teaching English as a foreign language to over 25,000 people from 130 countries. In the United Kingdom, there are six residential language schools. The Bell School at Saffron Walden offers language courses for beginners through advanced levels, ranging from young learners to company executives. Saffron Walden is a small town in southeast England. It is popular with language learners because it offers a quiet educational environment for learning English, yet it is only a one-hour train ride north of London.

The school in Saffron Walden has excellent teaching facilities, including a self-access center (SAC) where learners are encouraged to go to take control of their language learning. They decide which skills to practice, which activities to do, how long to spend on an activity, and how to evaluate their learning. The SAC houses a large variety of language-learning materials covering all four skills plus examination practice packages. Learners can use the SAC for serious study purposes or for entertainment – chatting with classmates from different countries, watching videos, or reading magazines or newspapers.

During the introduction to new learners at the school, the class teacher takes the students to the SAC and gives them a tour of the facility. They then spend some class time in the SAC with their teacher becoming familiar with the materials and finding out what they can do there. After this introduction, the class is timetabled into the SAC for an hour and a half per week. During this time, they go to the SAC with their class teacher, where they might ask their teacher for suggestions of what they might do, check answers to worksheets, or chat. This nonformal teaching situation allows teachers and students to interact in a friendly manner, and it helps motivate students to see the value of their independent learning. Students may also use the SAC at lunch times or after class. Many students use the SAC, and it is frequently busy during the day with timetabled classes and in the evening, when it is used for more social purposes. In this way, the SAC is part of the language-learning culture of the school.

The school also takes students to the theater or musicals in London, and the SAC is often used for preparations for such visits.

8.5.2 Preparing for a Musical

Phantom of the Opera is a popular musical that many students choose to see while studying in England. To enable the students to appreciate the musical, the staff at the Bell School prepared a series of worksheets and activities that can be done in the SAC. The worksheets cover a variety of levels from elementary to upper intermediate. The following is a list of what is available for the students to choose from:

- Reading – *London's Haunted Theatres*; *Theatre Guide*
- Reader with cassette – *Phantom of the Opera* by Jennifer Bassett
- Listening – The story of *Phantom of the Opera* (in-house material)
- Songs (from the musical) – "The Phantom of the Opera," "Music of the Night," "Think of Me," "All I Ask of You," "Wishing You Were Somehow Here Again"
- Dictation (in-house published material) – The Phantom of the Opera (1); The Phantom of the Opera (2)

AIMS AND OBJECTIVES

General Aims. As can be seen from the contents, most of the materials aim at developing students' listening skills so that they can comprehend the musical when they see it.

Objectives. In terms of the materials, the objectives can be categorized thus: to gain an understanding of the story line of the musical, to understand as much of the songs' lyrics as possible, and to be able to follow fast speech for entertainment purposes.

8.5.3 Exercise Types

We will look at two of the worksheets students can attempt: (1) The Story of *Phantom of the Opera* and (2) The Song "Music of the Night."

Exercise 1 – The Story of *Phantom of the Opera*. Students collect a package of materials comprising a tape cassette, a transcript of the story, a worksheet, and an answer key. They then decide how they will use the materials. For example, the student might look at the worksheet first, gain an idea of what is expected from listening to the tape, listen to the tape, check true or false on the worksheet, and then check the answers from the key. If there are any problems, the student may consult the tape script.

Tapescript
Listening Comprehension
The *Phantom of the Opera* is one of the most successful musical productions in London – it is certainly one of the most dramatic!

The Phantom was first heard of in France and has been the subject of many stories ever since. Although the writer of the definitive story was a French author called Gaston Leroux, it was an English composer, Andrew Lloyd Webber, who took the narrative and set it to music.

The story is set in Paris in the late nineteenth century, and although the title contains the word *Phantom*, the main character is not really dead at all! He is a man who was born extremely ugly and wears a mask and a long flowing cloak to cover his ugliness. He is a very angry and unhappy man who hides away in the cellars underneath the theater, doing everything he can to hurt the people involved in the operas. He is bitter and frustrated and expresses his feelings through a fantastic musical ability. Then he falls in love with Christine, a young and beautiful opera singer who brings happiness to his life, and he trains her musical ability through magic. Unfortunately she doesn't know that he exists, and it is very sad that he loves her but cannot reach her. One day, feeling bitter about everything that has happened to him, and jealous of Christine's young handsome lover, the Phantom kidnaps her and takes her to his hideaway where he plans to share his music with her.

The story is both sad and frightening, and the production is excellent, with wonderful stage effects.

After writing *Phantom*, Andrew Lloyd Webber had many other successful shows including *Sunset Boulevard* and *Aspects of Love*, but the *Phantom* remains one of the most popular and is well worth seeing!

Worksheet

Listening

Listen to the tape and say whether the statements are TRUE or FALSE.

1. The *Phantom of the Opera* is a great success.
2. The story originates from Scotland.
3. The writer, Gaston Leroux, was from France.
4. The musical was written by Andrew Lloyd Webber.
5. The story is set in 1818 in Paris.
6. The story takes place in the London Opera House.
7. The Phantom isn't really a ghost.
8. The Phantom had an accident which made him ugly.
9. He wears a black tie and white suit.
10. The Phantom tries to help the people from the Opera House.
11. The Phantom is depressed about Christine.
12. The Phantom is bitter about his past.

13. The Phantom is a pitiful character.
14. Christine knows he lives behind the Opera House.
15. The Phantom kidnaps Christine.
16. It's a sad and frightening story.
17. Andrew Lloyd Weber also wrote *Crazy For You*.

Exercise 2 – The Song "Music of the Night." Students collect the package from the songs' section of *Phantom of the Opera*. In this package there is a tape cassette, a worksheet, and an answer key. Once again, students decide how to work though the material. One way is to first listen to the song for fun; they might even do this several times. Then they might look at the vocabulary list and check a dictionary for the meaning of the words. A student then might decide *not* to complete the gap-fill exercise, but rather follow the answer key and sing along with the song. Finally, the student might try the worksheet as a memory test.

Worksheet
Song: "Music of the Night"
This song is sung by the Phantom and explains how much he loves music and what it means to him.
   The following words are missing from the song. Check their meaning in a dictionary. Listen to the song and fill in the gaps. All the words are connected with the magical atmosphere of the musical.

deftly	soul	sense	savor
light	intoxication	imagination	power
sensation	give in	surrender	take flight
splendor	journey	garish	
possess	spirit	fantasies	

Night time sharpens
Heighten each _____
Darkness stirs and wakes the _____
Silently the senses abandon their defenses
Slowly, gently, night unfurls its _____
Grasp it, _____ it, tremulous and tender
Turn your face away from the _____ light of day
Turn your thought away from cold, unfeeling _____
And listen to the music of the night
Close your eyes and _____ to your darkest dreams

Purge your thoughts of the life you knew before
Close your eyes, let your _____ start to soar
And you'll live as you've never lived before
Softly, _____ music shall caress you
Feel it, breathe it, secretly _____ you
Open up your mind
Let your _____ unwind
In this darkness which you know you cannot fight
The darkness of the music of the night
Let your mind start a _____
Through a strange new world
Leave all thoughts of the life you knew before
Let your _____ take you where you long to be
Only then can you belong to me
Floating, holding, sweet _____
Touch me, trust me _____ each sensation
Let the dream begin
Let your darker side _____
To the power of the music that I write
The _____ of the music of the night
You alone can make my song _____
And help me make the music of the night.

8.5.4 Dimensions of the Model Covered in the Case Study

INDIVIDUALIZATION

Obviously, the whole context of self-access language learning is focused on empowering learners so that they can make decisions about their language learning (see Gardner and Miller 1999 for a comprehensive account of self-access language learning). Although the students in the Bell School are timetabled to use the SAC, they decide how to use it. The learning context of self-access means that students make decisions based on their own personal preferences. To a large extent the students must interact with the materials on their own. In the materials, there are instructions as to how to use them, but if learners choose to ignore this advice, that is their decision. By allowing the learners to use the materials in whatever way they wish, the dimension of individualization is fully catered to.

SOCIAL DIMENSION

As mentioned in the introduction, learners using the SAC need to interact with their tutors when they are first taken to the center. Then they attend the SAC as part of their timetabled classes. In addition, they can go in their free time. In each of these situations, the learners have an opportunity to engage in conversations with the tutors or with their classmates, allowing them to explore language use in a more social environment (i.e., not in the classroom, and not necessarily talking about classroom-based learning). This social dimension does not need to be built into self-access language learning (SALL) materials specifically, although if learners wanted to improve their oral/aural skills, a specific worksheet could be prepared to help them.

Self-access does not mean learning in isolation; in fact, most learners using SALL do so with other learners. By interacting with tutors and other learners in SACs, social dimensions of the model are developed.

CONTEXTUAL DIMENSION

The whole idea behind preparing students for attending a theater performance is to contextualize the event. There are many aspects of contextual dimensions to the SALL situation described earlier. Learners can become familiar with the story line and context of the musical by reading about it or by surveying the worksheets. Because all the worksheets are closely related to the topic of the musical, the learners can build up complex schemata in which to frame the musical they will eventually see and hear.

AFFECTIVE DIMENSION

The tutor often caters to affective dimensions in SALL by helping learners select materials, giving advice on how best to use the worksheets, and generally chatting with the student in an encouraging way. Affective dimensions can be built into SALL worksheets themselves by asking learners to take their emotional temperature from time to time, that is, by having students think about how they feel about learning from the material. This assessment has not, however, been done in the sample material presented previously. However, the use of songs to motivate learners is obvious here, and this certainly comes within the realm of affective dimensions.

STRATEGIC DIMENSION

Several strategies are suggested by the SALL material: Listening for specific information, using a dictionary, guessing unknown words, and relaxing and listening to songs. Although these strategies can be highlighted through the materials, it is up to the individual learner to decide how much to practice the strategies. Learners may also choose to employ their own strategies, as for example when the learner decides not to do the cloze exercise but to focus on listening to and singing along with the song.

8.5.5 Dimensions of the Model That Appear to Be Missing from the Case Study

CROSS-CULTURAL DIMENSION

The materials that help prepare students for their theater visit do not address any specific cross-cultural dimension. Students could, however, be asked to consider the whole concept of theater and compare the situation of a visit to the theater in London with their own culture of theater and maybe find out more about other learners' theatrical customs. For example, the worksheet on London's haunted theaters focuses the learners' attention on the history of the theater in London and on the many mysteries associated with theater life. Learners can then be encouraged to consider what they know about theatrical traditions in other countries, such as attitudes toward street theater, traditional versus contemporary theater, and significant events that have happened in theaters in their own countries – presidents assassinated or treaties signed.

INTERTEXTUAL DIMENSION

The lack of any intertextual dimension to the preparation for visiting *Phantom of the Opera* might be corrected by directing students toward reading and analyzing poetry. In poetry, for instance, students can become aware of rhyming, collocations, alliteration, rhythm, and imagery, among other things, which would help prepare them for listening to a musical.

CRITICAL DIMENSION

One of the main themes of *Phantom of the Opera* is how the opera singer overcomes her horror of the musician's physical deformity and falls in love with him. This issue could be highlighted in worksheets in the SAC about how society reacts to, and often discriminates against, people who have some type of physical deformity. The topic could be exploited in a number of ways in the SAC: group discussions, video viewing of documentaries about burns victims, newspaper articles about the disabled, and so on.

8.5.6 Discussion

1. Preparing students for a theater visit may be considered as an out-of-class project. Do you involve your students in project work? Discuss the types of projects you have your students work on and how you think it helps them develop their listening skills.
2. Look at the dimensions of the model that *are* implicit in this case study. Do you agree with our analysis? What are some other ways in which the types of materials presented here help students develop their academic listening?
3. Look at the dimensions of the model that *are not* implicit in this case study. Discuss how you might introduce these dimensions into the teaching material.

8.6 Case Study 5 – An Intensive Language Course

8.6.1 The Setting

Northern Arizona University, in the United States, offers a Program in Intensive English (PIE) to international students who need to improve their English proficiency before registering in regular university classes. These students usually have TOEFL scores of between 360 and 540 and are required to undertake a full program of English prior to their studies. The program is also available to students who have met the university language requirement but who want additional English support. The students who take the PIE come from a variety of countries, such as Japan, Korea, China, Saudi Arabia, Mexico, and Russia. In addition to coping with their studies in English, they need to be able to live in an American society for the duration of their stay, so they need language skills for the classroom (e.g., listening to lectures, taking notes, talking with professors, writing term papers) and for any social and cultural situations they find themselves in outside of the classroom. Therefore, apart from helping students improve their overall language proficiency, the program also offers a course on Intercultural Communication, which specifically helps students develop their listening and speaking – the focus of this case study.

The English language program consists of a range of language and study skills for 26 contact hours per week. The courses last for 15 weeks during the academic year and 5 weeks during the summer. The program consists of the following components:

Course	Number of Hours Per Week
Core (integrated skills)	8
Writing	3
Reading	3
TOEFL	3
Pronunciation	3
Multimedia	2
Conversation (summer only)	2
Intercultural Communication (academic year only)	2
Total	26

8.6.2 Description of the Course

The Intercultural Communication (IC) class meets for two hours per week throughout the semester. This class has several special features.

- The focus is on listening/speaking.
- There are no homework assignments.
- All the topics of the classes are on cultural and cross-cultural issues.
- The class is made up of two-thirds language students and one-third MA-TESL students.

In the IC class, the only requirement of the students is that they attend class and participate. The reason there are no assignments and tests is that the course's aims are to sensitize students to issues of culture, to have them freely discuss issues that may be sensitive, and to try to foster a greater understanding of other people and their views of life. The effect of this class is that overseas students are better able to integrate into American society and cope with American university culture.

The MA-TESL students take the course for credit toward their final degree. Typically, half of them will be native-English speakers, and half nonnative-English speakers with TOEFL scores of above 570. Their participation in the IC class is twofold: (1) They are part of the class and interact with the overseas students as classmates, and (2) each MA-TESL student is required, under guidance, to lead a class each week and so gain experience in teaching. This unique combination of students and student teachers results in several goals being reached:

- Overseas students are exposed to many different English speakers.
- Each group always has a nativelike speaker of English in it to advise on pronunciation and act as a good model.
- Overseas students are exposed to many different styles of teaching.

In addition to these pedagogical considerations, the overseas students in the program are exposed to a variety of views and opinions on topics, have a safe platform from which to talk about their own views and opinions, and develop friendships that they maintain throughout their time at Northern Arizona University because of the nonthreatening academic environment.

A typical two-hour lesson is divided into five sections: presentation of topic – whole class; group or pair work; regroup or combine groups (e.g., pyramid discussion); break; continued group work; whole class discussion and closure.

Because of the nature of the class and the different profiles and interests of each group, the topics are not set for the course in advance. After the first two sessions have been conducted by the master teacher (i.e., the staff member who is in charge of the course), each MA-TESL student teacher, under guidance from the master teacher, is allowed to choose a topic of interest. The topics are usually "safe" to begin with – holidays, food – but progress to more controversial issues, such as cultural stereotypes, politics, and culture shock.

AIMS AND OBJECTIVES

General Aims. The general aim is to provide students in the PIE with an opportunity to practice informal listening and speaking while exploring culturally relevant topics. This course is designed to help students communicate effectively and to adjust to the cultural norms of American university life.

Objectives. Upon completing this course students will

- be comfortable interacting with individuals and groups.
- have an increased understanding of American culture.
- have an increased awareness of other cultures and norms.
- have an awareness of American conversational norms.
- have strategies to repair communication breakdowns.

Table 8.1 *Example of Handout and Poster*

	Saudi Arabian	Mexican	Korean	American	Dutch	Malaysian
Favorite food						
Favorite drinks						
Favorite sports						
Favorite pastime						
Popular clothing						
Typical house						
Behavior or manners						
Most important thing						

SAMPLE LESSON – STEREOTYPES

The following lesson outline is based on the topic of stereotypes. It comes midway through the course, when the students are comfortable with the course format and with talking to one another about sensitive issues.

Lesson Goals: To share aspects of one another's cultures; to practice listening and speaking in small and large groups

Materials: Talking stick (a decorated stick), atlases, handout, poster (same as handout, see Table 8.1), and markers

Classroom Setup: Chairs in a circle. Poster displayed on board (see following example)

Warm-up Activity (15–20 minutes)

Purpose: To share how each of us is a part of our culture.

Procedure: The entire group is seated in a circle with the teacher holding the talking stick. If the class has more than 20 students, the teacher might want to make two circles.

1. The teacher introduces the topic of getting to know about other cultures and refers to the poster on the board.
2. The teacher explains how some Native American tribes use a talking stick to allow people to speak. If you have the stick, you can talk. The stick is passed to those wishing to speak.
3. The teacher explains that each person will take a turn to tell something about himself/herself that is cultural or that may be culturally determined and may make them different from others in the room.
4. The teacher passes the talking stick to someone in the circle, and that person shares something and then passes the stick to someone else.

Activity 1 (20–30 minutes)
Purpose: To explore stereotypes.
Procedure: Students sit in small groups of two or three and try to fill in as many boxes on their handouts as possible. In some instances, they will be recalling what was just said by a speaker using the talking stick; in other cases they might discuss together what they think they know about a certain cultural group and then fill in their handouts.
Break (15 minutes)
This class always has a break to allow the students to mingle and interact. Tea and cookies are available during the break.

Activity 2 (15–20 minutes)
Purpose: To discuss stereotypes.
Procedure:

1. Students get into assigned groups. The teacher has made a list of groups ahead of time. Each group has as many different countries represented as possible, given the class composition. Having the teacher assign groups allows the teacher to consider personality and language proficiency and to make sure that one MA-TESL student is in each group.
2. In groups, the students discuss the "answers" for their countries and where their ideas may have originated. Some questions that can be discussed include these: Are these accurate stereotypes? How did these stereotypes come about? Were your "answers" about your own country different from those of other students? Why is that?

Activity 3 (15–20 minutes)
Purpose: To continue discussion of stereotypes.
Procedure:

1. Students are rearranged into different groups to share their information.
2. At the same time, students are encouraged to go to the board and fill in the poster with the "correct" information about their cultural group.

Closure (10–15 minutes)
Purpose: To provide closure to the topic of stereotypes; to allow for whole class discussion.

Procedure:

1. Students return to the circle that began the class.
2. Using the talking stick, students share what they learned about other countries and how their countries are perceived. The notion of stereo-types is discussed for its positive and negative aspects.

8.6.3 Dimensions of Listening Covered in This Case Study

INDIVIDUALIZATION

The topic relates directly to who is in the class. The students are the experts about their own countries and cultures. Furthermore, students get practice interacting in both small and large groups and can take part in the lesson as much as they wish.

CONTEXTUAL DIMENSION

The listening activities are contextualized because all students have prior knowledge from a variety of sources that is relevant to the topic for discussion. There is also the handout and supporting poster, which students can use as a frame of reference while listening to others talk about their cultures.

AFFECTIVE DIMENSION

Because students are speaking about and listening to topics within their personal knowledge, there is an affective dimension to the lesson. This, though, needs to be handled carefully in such a course because the students' reactions to the topic can become emotional. Learning how to interact without overreacting is important here. For instance, in the lesson, a student may hear something he/she does not like or agree with. By extending the discussion students may learn how to monitor their emotions and how to react to the information about stereotypes.

STRATEGIC DIMENSIONS

Because of the nurturing nature of the class, students with less language proficiency have an opportunity to explore how to communicate their ideas. They can explore listening and speaking strategies in a friendly environment that they can later use outside the classroom.

CROSS-CULTURAL DIMENSION

The whole course is oriented around the cross-cultural dimension. The lesson on stereotypes is a good example of exploring cross-cultural issues.

SOCIAL DIMENSION

The nature of the class is social. In addition to using a range of classroom social norms (e.g., small group, pair work discussion, and individual participation in the lesson), the students have a break time for social interaction. This interaction is necessarily conducted in English because of the composition of the class.

CRITICAL DIMENSION

Students are asked to think critically and to examine both how they constructed the stereotypes of the other countries and how others constructed stereotypes of their countries. Student also learn how to listen and interact in situations that might be perceived as critical.

8.6.4 Dimensions of Listening Not Covered in This Case Study

INTERTEXTUAL DIMENSION

The intertextual dimension is not prominent in the stereotypes lesson. However, if the lesson were on advertising in different countries, for instance, this dimension might also be covered in the course because students would need to rely on their knowledge of different types of texts and the messages they carry to illustrate their points.

8.6.5 Discussion

1. Do you teach or have you been a student in a lesson on cultural differences? What listening problems can occur in such lessons?
2. This course is conducted with multilingual groups. What problems might you encounter having a similar lesson with a monolingual group? How could you overcome some of these problems?
3. If you were conducting the same lesson on stereotypes with a homogenous group, which of the listening dimensions might you have problems with? Explain.

4. The intertextual dimension is the only listening dimension that is not covered in the stereotype lesson. Develop a way to introduce this dimension to the lesson.

Task 1

Write a case study of a listening course you are familiar with. Try to follow a format similar to that used for the cases in this chapter.

Introduction/setting
The course/aims and objectives
Example of materials/activities
Evaluation in terms of the eight dimensions of the pedagogical model

Present your case to a partner, talking him/her through it.

8.7 Conclusion

In this chapter, we attempted to bring to life some of the contexts in which learners develop their listening skills. As can be seen from the five case studies presented, many approaches can be taken to develop and improve listening in a second language. Some, like the primary school, are quite controled, whereas others, like the self-access center, allow learners to make choices for themselves. The secondary school context illustrates how technology can aid the development of listening skills outside the classroom, while the ESL case study shows how courses can be developed to heighten learners' awareness of critical and cultural issues through listening. The English for Science and Technology university case study highlights how even in a formal educational context there is room for learners to develop listening beyond what is normally expected in their lectures.

PART III:
KEY ISSUES IN TEACHING AND TESTING

In Part III, we present what we consider to be three key issues that all language teachers face when helping learners develop listening skills. At the end of each chapter, we comment on how the pedagogical model, presented in Part II, may assist teachers in better dealing with these key issues.

In Chapter 9, we investigate how technology is used to facilitate listening. In most language classes today, it is common for the teacher to use some form of technology, ranging from tape recorders to computers, in the listening lessons. Access to authentic listening material, or simply to a variety of recorded listening material, allows teachers opportunities to explore dimensions of the pedagogical model that they might not have been able to do otherwise.

Chapter 10 focuses on how listening is developed through the use of good questioning techniques. Variety in the use of questions helps stimulate learners' interest and aids the teacher in checking different levels of comprehension. Therefore, developing skills in the use of appropriate questions is of paramount importance for all language teachers. In Chapter 10, we review some of the questioning techniques teachers can use. We then focus on the different dimensions of the pedagogical model and suggest that each dimension needs different types of questions in order for students to be fully involved in developing their listening skills.

The final chapter of Part III is devoted to testing, the third of our "issues." We examine the various ways in which tests can be used to assess listening ability and conclude that a communicative approach is appropriate if teachers wish to use the pedagogical model presented in Part II and be able to test learners' abilities in each of the dimensions.

The book concludes with a set of essay questions, projects, and presentations designed to assess readers' understanding of various aspects of the book.

9 Developing Listening Skills Through Technology

9.1 Introduction

With the ever-increasing accessibility of technology and the fast pace at which technology is changing today, the styles and strategies of students' learning are also developing and expanding. In this chapter, we look at how using technology can help develop listening skills. First, we look at low-tech components: radio, tape recorders, and language laboratories. Then we examine the huge influence video has had in language teaching. This area we categorize as mid-tech. Finally, we explore some of the high-tech features of computer technology in and out of the classroom.

9.2 Radio

Listening to the radio is one of the most accessible ways a learner has of developing listening skills. Radios are low-tech, and radio broadcasts are continuous. Listening to the radio, however, is not an activity that is often used in class time. Perhaps this is because radio listening can be done only in real time, and the scheduling of language classes to catch particular radio programs is difficult. Furthermore, the difficulties of obtaining copyright often prevent teachers from recording from the radio for classroom use. But it is still a listening medium that offers many potential benefits for learners, some of which are outlined below.

Extensive listening practice. Perhaps because of the real-time listening aspect of the radio, one of the most important dimensions it has to offer learners is the experience of listening to nonstop language. Learners are able to develop an "ear" for the language and tune in and out whenever they wish.

Access to native speaker models. In many L2 contexts the only oral models student have are of nonnative speakers speaking English. These models are often preferred by students simply because the L2 speaker uses pronunciation features similar to those that the learners are accustomed to. However, to develop listening skills that will enable learners to comprehend foreigners, learners need exposure to different speakers of English. Radio broadcasts allow learners to listen to native speakers in a variety of contexts, from the news read in simple English (Voice of America and BBC both have such programs) to interviews on specific topics to phone-ins.

Specially produced language programs. Some of the main radio broadcasters produce excellent language programs with supplementary written materials of high quality. In addition, local radio stations produce their own special programs for learners. So it is not difficult to find a radio program to aid in language development (see Case Study 2, Chapter 8).

Access to information. In 1981, one of the authors was working in a provincial town in Egypt. On National Day, he went to visit a friend to watch the National Day procession on TV. However, when he arrived he was told that the TV coverage had blanked out because of the assassination of President Anwar Sadat. The whole family, most of whom did not understand English, were gathered around the radio listening to the BBC, while the eldest son translated the news of the assassination. Radio's ability to provide access to uncensored news helps people develop many of the critical skills that good listeners need in order to evaluate what they hear.

Opportunity to listen creatively to the L2. By using a radio, the "(listening) activity is telescoped by the ear but expanded by the eye" (Tomalin, 1986:10). This means that listeners must use their imaginations when they listen to the radio. For some learners, this can create worlds that are much more entertaining than the real world (e.g., the classroom).

Accessibility. Radios are more accessible than TV or video. Listening to the L2 over a radio is perhaps the most accessible form of listening practice most language students can have. Since the days of traditional approaches to language teaching (see Chapter 1), teachers have encouraged their students to "tune in" to stations such as Voice of America and the BBC. It is not uncommon to find language learners in remote areas tuning in to English radio stations in order to learn the language. And nowadays, with advances in technology, radios can even run without any electrical or main battery power source. A radio has been developed that works by winding up a power source in an internal battery. When the battery runs down, the user simply winds it up again.

Convenience. Students can use small personal radios to listen wherever and whenever they wish. The digitalization of transistors has resulted in the availability of very small radios with excellent sound quality. This allows listeners to take their radios anywhere they like, and they can tune in via small earpieces so as not to disturb others nearby.

Motivation of locally produced radio programs. In one case study in Chapter 8, we illustrated how local radio programs can motivate students to listen. This heightened motivation results in regular listening habits that help students develop good listening skills.

Entertainment. One of the main reasons people listen to radios is for entertainment. Learners tune in to their favorite programs or listen to pop songs. This differentiates radio listening from classroom-based listening, which is often test oriented.

9.2.1 Using Radio to Practice Listening

Many teachers like to help their students develop general or specific listening skills via the radio. The most efficient materials teachers can produce to help their students are generic worksheets, since teachers cannot predict what the content of a news program or story will be. The worksheet in Figure 9.1 illustrates a generic activity that learners may use while listening to any news program on the radio. As can be seen, the teacher needs to produce only one version of the worksheet, but the students can use it many times. This is an efficient use of the teacher's time and provides a useful resource for students to learn from.

Task 1
Produce a generic worksheet for one of the following types of radio programs: the weather forecast, a sports program, top ten hits (a music program), an interview.

9.3 Audio tapes

Audiocassette players are the simplest and cheapest way to provide listening practice opportunities for students in a classroom. Because nearly all

---

Listening to the News

Objective:

To listen and gather as much information about the news on radio as possible.

What you need:

a radio tuned in to an English language station
paper and pen
a copy of today's newspaper

What you need to do:

1. Tune in to the news on the radio. (Aim to listen on the hour, as that is usually when most stations broadcast the news.)

2. While you listen, make notes on the main stories. Do not worry about understanding everything; focus on the main points of the news.

3. After listening to the news, review your notes and add anything you might have heard but did not make a note of.

4. Now check if the stories you heard on the radio are also reported in the daily newspaper. If they are, read the newspaper stories and find out if your notes resemble the articles.

Remember:

You may find this activity challenging the first time you do it. However, if you do it often enough, you will understand more of the radio news.

Figure 9.1 A generic worksheet for listening to the news

general course books these days have accompanying audiocassettes, a cassette player has become an essential tool in the language classroom. The following are some of the reasons using audiotapes enhances listening in class. We illustrate each point with a classroom activity students may be required to do.

Extensive listening practice. Students can practice their extensive listening in a variety of ways. That is, they listen to extended stretches of discourse in a directed fashion, as opposed to out-of-class extensive listening, usually for fun (e.g., movies). Many of the situations in which students need to use extensive listening skills require them to listen to unfamiliar speakers or to a variety of speakers. Without the aid of audiotapes, teachers can only do so much to create listening contexts for students to have extensive listening practice. With the help of tapes, teachers are able to create some of the following situations so that students can acquire overall comprehension skills:

- Guessing the general meaning from spoken text and gathering information in order to do something.

Activity A
Listen to the tape of three people having a discussion about pollution. Try to get a general impression of how they feel about the problems. As you listen, consider whose opinions you like most.

- Listening for pleasure.

Activity B
Listen to this song. Have you heard it before? Do you like it? You can listen just for fun, or you can follow the song's words on page 37 of your student book.

- Attending to fast speech.

Activity C
Sometimes we find it difficult to listen because the speaker is speaking very fast. Listen to this tape and at the end decide how much, from 0 to 100 percent, you understood.

- Distinguishing among a variety of voices.

Activity D
We are going to listen to a tape in which speakers from different countries are talking. Try to identify which country the speaker is from by the way he/she speaks. Were any speakers more understandable then others? What made them more understandable?

Intensive listening practice. Replaying a tape several times allows students the opportunity to focus on discrete points of the language and to develop intensive listening skills. If this is the purpose of the activity, then the teacher should state this at the onset and then be prepared to play the tape more than once. However, teachers need to be aware that some students can become dependent on repetitive listening to tapes before they are satisfied with their ability to comprehend any of the information, at either the specific or general level. We might call this the "play it again Sam" syndrome. That is, students request numerous replays of the tape because they think they have not heard everything. If the teacher allows the students to dictate the number of repetitions of the tape, then the pacing of lessons gets disrupted, and students focus more and more on what they think they have *not* heard, rather than be happy with what they have heard. Some common intensive listening practice activities include the following.

- Listening for key words.

Activity E
Listen to the tape and see if you can hear the words on the board (a vocabulary list has been generated from the previous stage in the lesson).

- Listening to pronunciation and intonation patterns.

Activity F
Listen to these two people talking. Listen to how Mary asks the questions. Does her voice go up or down at the end of the sentence?

- Listening to contracted forms.

Activity G
Listen to how the people on the tape say the following: *he'd, I'd, we'll, couldn't.*

- Listening to complete a classroom task (true/false, questions, picture matching).

Activity H
Look at the pictures on page 54 of your textbook. There are eight pictures. Listen to the tape and decide which picture is being described. Listen for the vocabulary that will help you match the picture.

- Practicing listen-and-repeat drills.

Activity I
Listen to these sentences. After you hear each sentence, repeat it.
She's going on holiday, isn't she?
He's 54 in August, isn't he?
They're happy living in Boston, aren't they?
etc.

Task 2

Examine a listening textbook you are familiar with. Look at the taped exercises and decide whether they are intended to help students develop extensive or intensive listening skills. Do you think this is the best focus for the listening material?

Discuss your ideas with a partner.

9.4 Language Laboratory

With the advent of tape recorders in the 1950s and the rise of the audio-lingual method of teaching (see Chapter 1), language laboratories became popular facilities in many schools. The theory behind the audio-lingual method was that we are able to condition students to learn language. The best way to do this was thought to be by way of mechanical drills. Theoretically, if students heard and repeated language structures often enough, they would learn the language better. Typical drills performed in the language laboratory took the form of repetition drills or substitution drills.

A Repetition Drill

Tape:	The man went for a walk.
Student:	The man went for a walk.
Tape:	The lady went for a swim.
Student:	The lady went for a swim.

A Substitution Drill

Tape:	The man went for a walk. 'Lady'
Student:	The lady went for a walk.
Tape:	'Swim.'
Student:	The lady went for a swim.

It did not take long for many students to become turned off by such repetitions. The lack of quality materials and the boredom factor for both students and teachers resulted in language laboratories going out of fashion. Another reason for the language laboratory's demise was the advent of new teaching methods that focused less on drilling and more on the communicative aspects of language.

In the past decade or so, language laboratories have been making something of a comeback in developing listening skills. This is because

(1) material writers have produced quality materials that can be used in the laboratory, and (2) students have been encouraged to take more responsibility for their learning, and they can control the type of listening exercises they wish to do in the language laboratory, which in many institutions has taken on features of a self-access center (see Gardner and Miller 1999). An example of quality materials that can be used in the language laboratory is the *Headway, Pronunciation* series (Bowler and Cunningham 1991).

9.5 Video

The use of video to help develop listening skills has received much attention since it began to appear regularly in language classes in the mid 1970s. The obvious contextualization of language provided by video made it a popular medium in non-English-speaking countries (see Baltova 1994). Over the past two decades, researchers have shown that many other facets make video useful to language learners. Some of these are that video often promotes the motivation to listen; it provides a rich context for authenticity of language use; the paralinguistic features of spoken text become available to the learners (compared with radio, that is); and it aids learners' understanding of the cultural contexts in which the language is used.

ACTIVE VIEWING

Throughout this book we have made the case for listening to be treated as an active process. Video viewing, however, can be a relatively passive activity and still benefit the listeners. Most often this type of viewing is done at home, or as part of private study time. Active viewing is what is most frequently promoted in the classroom setting. Both active and less active viewing of videos are beneficial in helping learners develop their listening skills. When using video in the language class, the teacher must take on some new and important roles. For instance, apart from selecting the video material and supporting materials (something which the teacher may be expected to do in any situation), the teacher must decide how to integrate the video into the lesson and what types of listening skills the video encourages. In addition, the teacher must learn how to control the video playback facilities in order for the learners to focus on the video material and not on watching the teacher try to solve technical problems. The type of follow-up activities and tasks is also an important issue for the teachers to consider in order to exploit the material. Learners also have a change in roles when viewing video material. They need to become participants in the process of listening

Title of video: Around the World in 15 Minutes – Canada

Read over the following questions; then watch the video and choose the correct answer.

1. The population of Canada is
   (a) 12 million   (b) 25 million   (c) 250 million

2. The best way to travel to Canada's north is by
   (a) car   (b) train   (c) plane

3. The Northwest Territories covers
   (a) 0.5 million   (b) 1.5 million   (c) 15 million square miles.

4. Why did white men originally come to the Northwest Territories?
   (a) to open schools   (b) to mine for gold   (c) to bring religion

5. On what date is the end of the winter celebrated?
   (a) March 28th (b) March 21st (c) March 25th

6. How many hours of daylight are there during summer days?
   (a) 18–20   (b) 8–10   (c) 2

7. How many provinces are there in Canada?
   (a) 2   (b) 10   (c) 18

8. How many people attend the Calgary Stampede daily?
   (a) 50,000   (b) 15,000   (c) 5,000

9. What were the chuck wagons originally used for?
   (a) racing   (b) food   (c) carrying people

10. Who can earn up to $75,000?
    (a) Indians   (b) drivers   (c) miners

Figure 9.2 An active viewing worksheet (adapted from the ELC self-access materials at City University of Hong Kong)

and to engage in the pre-, while-, and postviewing activities in order to develop their listening skills. Figure 9.2 shows an example of an active viewing worksheet to accompany a video on Canada (*Around the World in 15 Minutes*).

Task 3

Consider a popular comedy program your students have easy access to. Construct an active viewing task, similar to that in Figure 9.2, that your students can do while watching this program.

VIEWING FOR PLEASURE

Often, viewing of videos is related to listening for pleasure, as in watching a movie. Studies in the L1 context have shown that viewing a movie for pleasure can be as effective as actively viewing it. Kenelfield (1977) set up a video lesson whereby one class was allowed to view a movie for entertainment while another group of learners was required to complete tasks in a more educational setting while viewing the same movie. As Kenelfield states: "There was no evidence that the entertainment group learned or understood less than the educational group." The difference, though, lay in the feedback. Learners who had watched the movie in a relaxed atmosphere tended to give more personalized accounts of what they saw, whereas the learners who watched under classroom conditions gave more factual and content-oriented accounts. However, students are often unaware of the benefits they can derive from viewing videos for pleasure. Many students consider viewing a movie for fun as a nonlistening activity. Gardner and Miller, in an extensive survey of independent learning facilities in Hong Kong (Gardner and Miller 1997), observed that many ESL students used their private study time by watching movies in English. However, when asked what they did with their study time, few of the students admitted to watching videos. When questioned later about this, the students admitted that they thought watching movies "didn't count" as a language-learning activity.

When suggesting movies for students to view, teachers need to be aware of some potential problems concerning content. Garis (1997) provides an overview of some of the problems in choosing appropriate movies. Such things as sex and nudity, violence, profanity and slang, and controversial issues may all cause offense to some learners. If the purpose of viewing the video is to use this activity for classroom discussions, then careful selection of the movie with the intended audience in mind is required; otherwise, previewing sessions that deal with some of the more controversial elements in the movie may allow students to decide whether they wish to view it. Listening may be severely hampered by students tuning out if they are shocked by the content of a movie.

General viewing of videos can be exploited later, after watching the movie for fun. Learners can be encouraged to employ their extensive listening skills by having group discussions, in or out of class, after watching a particular movie. In addition, generic worksheets may be developed to help those students who would like more focused attention when watching movies in an L2. Figure 9.3 is an example of the type of sections that might make up a generic worksheet to use when watching movies.

Name of movie: _____

Kind of movie: comedy/romance/drama/horror/action/science fiction/other

Names of main characters in the movie:

Male	Female	Animal	Other
_____	_____	_____	_____
_____	_____	_____	_____
_____	_____	_____	_____
_____	_____	_____	_____

Setting:

Where does the movie take place?

_____

Does the setting change during the movie?

_____

What is the main theme of the movie?

(a) relationships   (b) religion   (c) politics   (d) love   (e) survival   (f) other

Write a summary (around 50 words) to express how you felt while watching this movie.

_____

_____

_____

_____

_____

_____

After watching the movie, talk to a friend about it. See if they agree with your perceptions and feelings about the movie.

Figure 9.3 A generic worksheet for use when watching movies

Task 4

Prepare a generic worksheet, similar to that in Figure 9.3, which would aid students in following a television quiz show.

INTEGRATED VIEWING

Until recently, it was difficult to use television programs in the language class. The programs had to be viewed when they were broadcast because recording and replaying them sometimes infringed copyright laws. Furthermore, off-air television was sometimes rather difficult for many low-level learners, and it also had to be viewed while it was being transmitted, as opposed to watching a video recording, which could be paused and replayed. Recently, however, broadcasting companies have produced video packages of their programs that are intended for language learning/teaching purposes. The ABC News ESL Video Library is such a package and helps the learner integrate passive viewing with active viewing.

Focus on American Culture (Henly 1993) is part of the Focus on America series. In this package, which consists of a video, a student's book, and a teacher's booklet, students are exposed to U.S. culture as it appears on local news broadcasts. The four units in the series cover family, work, education, and trends in America. Within each unit are two to three segments that can be treated as individual lessons. Each lesson follows a similar format. The lesson begins with a Previewing section. Here students' schemata are activated via general discussion questions, and essential vocabulary is presented. The Global Viewing section aims at getting students to relax and enjoy viewing the video segment (passive viewing). In this part, students may focus on some global questions that will help them understand the main point in the segment. Next is the Intensive Viewing segment. Students view the segment again, and this time they listen for details (active viewing) and relate their listening to other tasks – note taking, cloze-type exercises, and ticking boxes. After this type of listening, there is a Language Focus section in each unit. In this part of the lesson, the teacher can highlight some particular grammatical structure or vocabulary that occurred in the video. Last, there is a Post Viewing section. This allows the students to use the information from the video to engage in discussions or do some other activity, such as complete a graph.

As can be seen from this outline, the aim of the Focus on America video series is to attempt to get learners to develop their extensive and intensive listening skills by way of authentic television programs and a structured format.

TYPES OF VIDEO MATERIAL

Different types of video material can be used to develop listening. Table 9.1, drawing from ideas in Lonergan (1984), illustrates five of these and gives the advantages and disadvantages of each.

Table 9.1 *Some Types of Video to Promote Listening*

Types of Video Material	Advantages	Disadvantages
1. Video for language learning	• Videos can be fully exploited through teacher control. • New videos have high quality of visuals and sound. • Language in the video has been graded. • Videos have accompanying written materials.	• Language may be viewed by learners as unauthentic, as it has been specially prepared. • Videos can become dated quite quickly. • Videos are expensive to buy.
2. Video from domestic broadcasts	• Learners are exposed to authentic language. • The speakers in the video may be from the learners' own country so learners may tune in to the accent easily. • Learners can use this medium outside the classroom.	• The language level may be too high for learners and so demotivate them to try and listen. • For copyright reasons, it is difficult to record off-air programs and show them in class. Therefore, the viewing must be done in real time.
3. Documentary videos	• Documentary videos are helpful in tertiary-level contexts because learners can get extra information by seeing the pictures (e.g., the life of a whale for biology students).	• Voice-overs can prove very difficult and even hinder comprehension (see MacWilliam 1986). • Documentary videos are usually made for L1 listeners, so social and cultural contexts may not be explained.
4. Teacher-produced videos	• These can focus on students' specific needs (see Brennam and Woodbury Miller 1982). • If the teachers are the actors, then the learners may be familiar with their accents. • Teacher investment in making the videos may mean that they are used more.	• Unless a high level of technical support is given them, the videos may look and sound unprofessional. • Making videos is time consuming.
5. Student-generated videos	• These videos help learners integrate their listening skills with their other language skills because they need to produce something. • Students usually work in groups and so establish a support system to help one another. • Editing requires intensive listening skills (see Brennam and Woodbury Miller 1982).	• Students may require much assistance in learning about the technology before they can use it. • Teachers have to be on hand to ensure quality control. • Students may feel shy about speaking on film.

9.6 Computer-Assisted Language Learning

Since the 1960s, computers have been used in language education. During this forty-year period, the use of computers could be divided into three main stages: behaviorist computer-assisted language learning (CALL); communicative CALL; and integrative CALL (Warschauer and Healey 1998). Each of these stages corresponds to the available technological and the prevailing pedagogical theories.

Behaviorist CALL, as its name implies, was informed by behaviorist theory (see Chapter 1). The type of language exercises students were asked to perform via the computer was repetitive language drills. All the activities students could perform on the computer at this time were reading and writing based.

Communicative CALL was the next stage of computer use. This followed the pedagogical trend into communicative language learning. With the advent of personal computers, students could have greater freedom to engage in language learning activities in their own homes. The type of exercises focused more on the use of forms than on the mechanical manipulation of the forms. The focus was still very much on written texts.

Integrated CALL aims to "integrate various skills (e.g., listening. speaking, reading, and writing) and also integrate technology fully into the language learning process" (Warschauer and Healey 1998:58). Nowadays, teachers are encouraged to make learning a process that involves technology. Now, with the expansion of computer storage facilities, it is possible to download sound and video clips, which open up new opportunities for students to develop their listening skills.

The enormous potential of computers means that we need to consider what effect computers will have on language education, and specifically how we might encourage our learners to develop their listening skills via computers.

CD-ROM

A rapid increase in educational software has paralleled the rise in computer use in classroom education and for home study. In fact, the rate at which new software is released makes it difficult to recommend any particular packages, because what is "highly recommended" today will be obsolete tomorrow. CD-ROMs have the following advantages over audio and video technology:

- Online scripts are often available.
- Glossaries for audio and video programs are included.

- Language exercises often have immediate feedback capability built into them so that students can check their progress as they complete exercises.
- The programs are becoming more and more attractive.
- Students can customize their learning via certain programs.
- Facility with computers is a skill that many students wish to learn anyway, so using computers to develop their language abilities seems a natural extension.
- Computer programs can integrate various skills (e.g., listening, reading, and writing) via one application.

In addition to the above list of benefits, Warschauer and Healey (1998:59) suggest the following benefits of using computers in language education:

- Multimodal practice with feedback
- Individualization in a large class
- Pair and small-group work on projects, either collaboratively or competitively
- The fun factor
- Variety in the resources available and learning styles used
- Exploratory learning with large amounts of language data
- Real-life skill building in computer use

Keeping up with educational software is a new and demanding role for teachers. Teachers need to become familiar with the computers that their institutions have and that their students use at home. Some basic hardware questions that you must ask include: Are the operating systems of the software and hardware compatible? Is there enough memory (RAM) on the computer to run the program? Is there enough disc space? Does the computer have speakers? Are a sound card and a video card installed in the computer? In addition to these general hardware questions, Thompson (2000) lists some specific criteria for software that can be used to evaluate CD-ROM listening skills programs (see Table 9.2).

Although computers do appear to facilitate language learning in a new dimension, the skill of listening via computer programs has not been researched much yet. This is probably because computers with sound capabilities were not in widespread use until recently. One study, however, has been conducted into the effects of computer technology in developing listening (Brett 1997). In his comparative study of three media – audio, video, and multimedia – Brett discovered that ". . . performance on tasks showed more effective comprehension and recall while using multimedia than either audio or video plus pen and paper" (p. 39).

Table 9.2 *Some Criteria for the Evaluation of CD-ROM Listening Skills Programs*

To Evaluate	To Consider
Documentation	• Is there a discussion of the program's goals, design, and contents? • Is there a tutorial on the program's operation? • Is a demonstration lesson included? • Are there lesson plans for use in a course or guidance for individual use? • Are research results on effectiveness of the program available? • Is there information about independent reviews of the program?
Listening Tools	
Links to the written version of passage	• The whole passage • Sentence-by-sentence • Phrase-by-phrase • Word-by-word
Spoken glosses	• Monolingual • Bilingual • Hint-type
Written glosses	• Monolingual • Bilingual • Hint-type
Visual glosses	• Images • Graphics • Videos
What kinds of additional resources are available?	• On-line talking dictionary • On-line written dictionary • On-line reference grammar • Background information • Cultural notes
Listening Interface	
Ease of navigation	• Is navigation between audio, activities, glosses, and tools simple? • Is navigation between screens fast?
Playback control	• Can listeners control the speed of audio playback? • Can playback be stopped after each phrase? after each sentence?
Timing	• Is there enough time to complete activities?
Archiving	• Can user's work be saved? • Can user's work be printed out?

By I. Thompson, 2000. Reproduced by permission of Irene Thompson.

Task 5

Use the criteria listed in Table 9.2 to evaluate a CD-ROM listening program you are familiar with.

Table 9.3 *Guidelines for Evaluating Web Sites for ESL Learners*

Aspect	To Consider
Source evaluation:	Trustworthy source, author's credentials, email, organizational support, rated by known authority, metainformation, and bad grammar
Purpose:	Skills, objectives, scope of audience, and target level
Pedagogy:	Instruction, feedback, sensory input, interactivity, communicativeness, and context
Design/construction:	Content, revisitability, appearance, navigation, load speed, technical (HTML) quality, organization, structure, ease of navigation, interaction, distracting visual elements, reliability, dependability, functional design, working hyperlinks
Contents:	Accurate information, up-to-date, comprehensive, rounded story, audience & purpose, objectivity, fairness, reasonableness, moderateness, external consistency
Access:	Standard multimedia formats, does it require extra software or plug-ins, free, easy to reach or overloaded, download time
Learners' needs for developing language skills:	The overall pedagogical designs and features, how well does a Web site respond to learners' difficulties and needs in developing second language skill(s)?

From "Guidelines for Evaluating Web Sites for ESL Learners," by H. Chen, 1999, in *Information Technology and Multimedia in English Language Teaching*, edited by B. Morrison, D. Cruikshank, D. Gardner, J. James and K. Keobke. Reproduced by permission from Howard Chen.

THE WORLD WIDE WEB

The World Wide Web (WWW) is destined to become one of the most popular facilities available to students to access information and help in their language learning. "Part library, part publishing house, part telephone, part interactive television, the Web represents one of the most diverse and revolutionary media in human history" (Warschauer and Healey 1998:64). There is so much out there on the Web, though, that it may appear a daunting task for students to decide which sites to visit and what to do after they have accessed a site. Based on the work of Graus (1999) and Nelson (1997), Chen (1999) lists some guidelines for evaluating Web sites for ESL learners. (Table 9.3).

Most Web sites are not developed for language-learning purposes, and only recently have students been able to download audio and video clips from sites. However, with the ever-increasing demand for sites that nonnative English speakers can use, many broadcasting corporations are making their sites more accessible to them. Table 9.4 (from Chen 1999) lists some of these sites, with their Web addresses.

Table 9.4 *A Selection of Web Sites Allowing Access to Listening Material*

Site Name	URL
American Broadcasting Company (ABC)	*http://www.abc.com*
British Broadcasting Company (BBC)	*http://www.bbc.co.uk*
Columbia Broadcasting System (CBS)	*http://www.cbs.com*
Cable News Network (CNN)	*http://www.cnn.com*
Microsoft-National Broadcasting Company (MS NBC)	*http://www.msnbc.com*
National Public Radio (NPR)	*http://www.npr.org*
Public Broadcasting Service (PBS)	*http://www.pbs.org*
Realmedia Guide	*http://www.realguide.com*
Voice of American (VOA)	*http://www.voa.gov*
ESL listening sites	
ESL Café Guide: Listening	*http://www.eslcafe.com/search/listening*
Eviews: Accents in English	*http://www.eviews.net*
The English Listening Lounge	*http://www.englishlistening.com*

Task 6

Using the guidelines in Table 9.3, evaluate a Web site you are familiar with or one from Table 9.4.

9.7 Conclusion

In this chapter, we reviewed the technological support that can be used to help students develop their listening skills. These are radio, audiotapes, television, video, and computers. Each type of technology provides opportunities for students to explore their ranges of listening strategies and in some cases develop new strategies. In most language classes today, students have access to some form of technology, whether it be small transistor radios or interactive multimedia. This wider access allows for more emphasis on certain aspects of our model, such as cross-cultural, interactional, critical, and contextual dimensions of listening, to be developed. Along with the advancements in technology, teachers' roles in helping their students develop better listening skills have also changed. English language teachers in the twenty-first century need to be prepared to exploit old and new technologies in many different ways to meet the changing needs of their students.

9.8 Discussion

1. Which specially produced radio programs do you recommend that your students listen to? Describe the program and why you recommend it to your students.

2. Discuss the ways in which your students use the language laboratory to develop their listening skills. What benefits do you perceive that your students get from using the language lab?

3. Do you agree with the statement about watching movies that "passive viewing is not negative viewing"? Why?

4. Describe the process and the outcome of making a video in class with your students.

5. How motivated are your students to use CALL? Do you integrate this into your syllabus? Explain why or why not.

6. Critically analyze one form of technology you are familiar with in terms of the eight dimensions of the pedagogical model.

10 *The Role of Questions in the Teaching of Listening*

10.1 Introduction

A major aspect of any language-teaching methodology is how the teacher checks comprehension. Often, this is done by asking students questions based on the texts. In listening, there is no simple correlation between the student's answering a question correctly and the level of comprehension achieved by the student. As we will illustrate in this chapter, depending on the way the question is asked, and the type of response accepted, listeners can demonstrate a wide range of comprehension ability. Where it is clear that they have not understood, this provides an indication of where teaching intervention is needed. It is through the teacher's skillful use of different question types and formats that learners are guided to develop effective listening.

Teaching listening has often been confused with *testing* listening. As questioning plays a major role in listening tests, teachers have often focused on preparing learners for tests in class instead of helping them develop effective listening skills. While reading the rest of this chapter, the reader should keep in mind that we are talking about teaching listening, not testing listening. Testing listening skills is the subject of Chapter 11.

10.2 Models for Integrating Questions While Teaching Listening

In the early language-teaching methods, the focus was very much on finding out how much information the listener could recall through direct questioning. In this product approach (Figure 10.1), the spoken text was presented, listeners "paid attention" to the message, and they were asked questions to check their comprehension. If they did not respond correctly to the teacher's questions, the tape was often played again, and again. Some students were never happy with their ability to listen to the oral text and constantly wanted it replayed in case they had missed something. The teacher encouraged

---

Model 1

| Spoken Text → | Learner's Comprehension → | Questions and Answers |
| Input | | |

Figure 10.1 A product approach to using questions in listening

---

Model 2a

Prelistening	*Input*	*While-Listening*	*Postlistening*
Set Scene →	Spoken Text → Listening Comprehension → Questions and	
Focus Qs		Answers	
Focus Strategies			

Figure 10.2a A process approach to using questions in listening

---

Model 2b

Prelistening	*Input*	*While-Listening*	*Postlistening*
Set Scene →	Spoken Text → Listening Comprehension → Comprehension	
Focus Qs		Evaluation	
Focus Strategies		↓ ↓ ↓	
		Check Check Check	

Figure 10.2b Using questions to develop listening skills

this focus on repetition by not clearly stating at the onset of the task exactly what the students were supposed to listen for.

As methods for teaching English developed, a more focused approach to teaching listening emerged. In a second model (Figure 10.2a), the teacher sets the scene first and possibly gives students reasons to listen, i.e., the focus questions or strategies. Then, while the students listen, they can focus on parts of the message that eventually become part of the postlistening questioning activity. Whereas the first model is more like a test, the second model, or process approach, begins to help students develop their skills and strategies for listening.

In an adaptation of the second model (Figure 10.2b), the teacher may set up comprehension-checking activities that would help learners monitor their understanding of the text. These types of *while-listening* activities not only help the learner follow the text, but also highlight where problems might exist. A variety of questioning techniques can be used throughout these checking phases. The outcome of this method is that, by the end of the listening period, the learners are *evaluating* their comprehension more than testing any ability to remember aspects of the text. The main difference between models 1 and 2 is that in model 1 the focus is only on postlistening questioning and is *product-based*, whereas in model 2 the *process* of listening is considered with the pre- and while-listening questions.

Task 1
Examine one exercise from a listening textbook. First prepare the exercise to fit with model 1; in other words, prepare a list of questions that can be asked after students have heard the text. Then, with the same listening exercise, try to prepare questions based on model 2a or 2b. Consider which comprehension skills are developed in each approach.

10.3 Question Types

10.3.1 Display Versus Referential

One of the most important distinctions to be made in regarding the types of questions asked during listening comprehension activities is between display and referential questions. A display question asks the learner to tell the teacher something that the teacher already knows. For example,

Q: How many people are having the discussion?
A: 3 (The teacher knows this and there is no other correct answer.)

This type of question is asked for several reasons:

- To ease the learner into the listening activity. (Display questions are often easier than referential questions.)
- To check basic understanding before proceeding to more complex issues in the text.
- To motivate weaker learners to take part in the lesson.

Table 10.1 *Display and Referential Types of Questions*

Display Questions	Referential Questions
Short answer	Open answers
Yes/no questions	Summarizing
True/false	Retelling (Note: The teacher does not know *how* the
Multiple choice	student will summarize or retell, and these
Gap-filling	retellings may be done in a number of ways.)
Information transfer	
Rearranging pictures	

Referential questions are questions to which the teachers does not have a definite answer. For example,

Q: How do you think Mary felt when she saw her house had been burgled?

The learner can answer in a variety of ways. Although the teacher may be able to predict some of the types of answers that might be given, it is up to the learner to choose how to answer the question. Table 10.1 shows the types of questions often associated with display and referential questions.

Task 2

Look at one unit from a general textbook. Identify all the listening exercises (there may be more than you think) and examine the types of questions that accompany them. Make a table to show how many display and how many referential questions are in the unit.

10.3.2 Focused Versus Open

In some situations, the teacher will help the learners focus on the details of the listening text so as to encourage more discrete listening strategies. Here, the questioning is *focused*. For instance, if the teacher wished to help learners develop the ability to discriminate between /p/ and /b/, a simple, minimal pair task could be set up where the teacher asks learners to say if the word in the text has a /p/ or a /b/ sound. The general question would be "What's the sound?" Or, if the two sounds are written on the board, "Is it the sound in column 1 or column 2?" Questioning like this helps focus the learners' attention on specific aspects of the text, which may otherwise be missed, or may be of use later on in the listening task.

Table 10.2 *Advantages and Disadvantages of Using Focused and Open Questions*

Type of Question	Advantages	Disadvantages
Focused questions	• They help learners focus on discrete item processing. • They alert learners to possible problems in pronunciation. • They give learners a sense of achievement, as they usually have only one correct answer. • They help learners focus attention on form.	• They need to be prepared in advance. • They are sometimes overused, so the learners lose the overall sense of the oral text. • They promote the "play-it-again-Sam" syndrome (i.e., students are never happy with their comprehension and ask for many repeats of text). • They do not usually portray how we listen in our L1, unless in special circumstances like taking a message on the telephone.
Open questions	• They are easy for the teacher to devise. • They can be used at any part of the listening activity. • They require more effort on the part of the learner. • They can liven up a lesson. • They allow learners to take some control of their learning. • They show the learner that his/her responses are valued by the teacher.	• They often do not have any correct answer. • They require creative thinking, which some students may find difficult in the L2. • They may result in no answer from shy learners. • They might slow the pace of the lesson down if learners disagree on an answer.

Open listening is likely to follow when a teacher asks learners to try to grasp the overall picture of a text. For example, the teacher says, "Listen to how Jerry talks about his holiday. Why do you think he enjoyed it so much?" The learner may continue to use focused listening strategies to answer this question if specific words from the text are used in the answer, but the student is also free to infer meaning from the tone of Jerry's voice and to use imagination in answering the question. Open listening activities often help learners develop overall general listening strategies, and these types of questions often have more than one correct answer. There are advantages and disadvantages to using both focused and open questions (see Table 10.2).

Focused and open questions are often used in conjunction with an oral text, although it is more common to find more focused questions in lower language level activities and more open questions in higher levels. This may be because learners at higher levels can express themselves in the target language more easily and hence are more likely to be able to answer open listening questions.

Task 3

Take any activity from a listening textbook. What kind of listening does the activity help the learners develop? Use the information in Table 10.2 to reflect on the effectiveness of the activity. Discuss your ideas with a partner.

10.3.3 Pre-, While-, and Postlistening Questions

The type of questions asked in a listening-based lesson very often depends on the stage of the lesson. There are three main phases in a listening lesson:

1. Prelistening – preparing students to achieve the most from listening.
2. While-listening – challenging and guiding students to handle the information and attitudes of the speakers during the listening.
3. Postlistening – reflecting on the language of the listening (sounds, grammar, vocabulary, inferencing, etc.) and applying understanding and interpretation.

With prelistening questions, the teacher is usually trying to get students ready for the listening activity. Here, both closed and open types of questions can be used to activate the students' schemata for the while-listening part of the lesson. The types of questions here will focus on

- eliciting background knowledge that may help in contextualizing the listening;
- checking whether pictures or diagrams are understood;
- checking whether students understand how the while-listening activity should be done.

The level of preparation and checking questions will vary depending on the level of the students and activity difficulty. In intermediate listening activity on, say, travel, the teacher may use some of the follow types of questions:

Q1: Has anyone traveled to Spain before? (open)
Q2: What was it like? (open)
Q3: Who else has traveled to Spain? (open)
Q4: Can you tell the class what it was like? (open)

Look at the picture on page 8 of your textbook (picture of a flamenco dancer).

Q5: What can you see in the picture? (focused)
Q6: What is she wearing? (focused)
Q7: Can you describe what the man is wearing? (focused)

We are going to listen to Virginia, who has just returned from a holiday in Spain. Let's listen to what interesting things she saw and did. While you listen, make some notes to remind yourself later.

Q8:   What will you listen for when I play the tape? (focused)
Q9:   Will you write down everything Virginia did on her holiday? (focused)
Q10: Why are you going to make notes? (focused)

During the while-listening section of the lesson, the students' attention is directed toward the activity. The type of questions the teacher asks here will guide students to develop either their focused or general listening skills. Not all the information in a listening activity needs a question. Indeed, if a teacher attempts to exploit fully all the listening activities in a textbook, there will be little time left in a language course for any other skill development.

Teachers commonly play a tape or video more than once for students. At each playing, different types of questions may be asked. For instance, in our listening lesson of Virginia's trip to Spain, the teacher may play the tape twice: once for the students to listen and make notes about Virginia's experiences, and a second time for them to check their notes.

Listen to Virginia talking about her trip to Spain.

Q11: Do you think she enjoyed herself or not? (open)

Now listen again to the tape and try to make some notes.

Q12: What things did she enjoy? What things did she not enjoy? (focused)

In the postlistening section of a lesson, the teacher attempts to exploit and extend the information the students heard in the while-listening section of the lesson. The questions here generally are more open or referential, with the intention of using the information in a more individual way.

Q13: So who has not been to Spain but would like to go there now? Why would you like to visit Spain? (open)
Q14: Would you visit the same places as Virginia visited? (open)

Task 4

Look at a listening activity and decide on the types of questions that can be asked in the pre-, while-, or postlistening stages of the lesson. If the activity already has specified questions, decide whether they are closed or open questions and what kind of replies you would expect from students.

10.3.4 First Language Versus Second Language

If learners in a class have the same language background, and if the teacher shares the L1 with the class, some consideration should be given to whether the learners should be allowed to answer questions in their L1. If, as mentioned in section 10.3.2, extensive questions are used more with learners at upper language levels because those students can express themselves more easily in the target language, what might result if we removed the L2 barrier for lower level students? We should consider asking these students more extensive questions in class also.

Language teaching methods have at various points in their development tried to use the target language exclusively. But the reality of most language teaching situations is that nonnative English teachers teach homogenous groups of learners. In such circumstances, it might be appropriate to allow learners to use their mother tongue to express what they understand in second language listening tasks.

Task 5

Look again at the exercises you examined in Task 2. What would be the effect if you allowed the students to answer the questions in their L1 (assuming, of course, that you also speak their L1)?

10.3.5 Form Versus Function

Sometimes teachers will want to focus the learners' attention on the language form (e.g., regular and irregular past tenses) in a listening task; at other times, on the language function (e.g., how requests are made). In a situation where understanding the relationship of time is an issue to comprehension, it is appropriate to ask some type of form question. For example,

Listen to the tape and tell me if Mary still drives a red car.

(In the tape it states that she *drove* a red car for many years.) Some early methods of language teaching suggested that learners should not be "given" the rules of the language but should guess their meaning through listening to the context. There are, however, many instances in oral texts where the learners' comprehension of grammar is important to the overall comprehension to the text. To constantly challenge the learners to try to work out the rules for themselves is to set up extra barriers to their learning and possibly slow down the comprehension process.

Focusing on the structure of the language all the time, though, would result in boring listening exercises. In some cases where authentic spoken text is used, it might also result in more confusion than is necessary (see the differences between spoken and written texts in Chapter 4). When listening to get an overall impression of a scene, or when listening for fun, the questions the teacher might ask could have more to do with the function of the language (or paralanguage) than with the structure of the text itself. The following are questions that focus on function:

Q: Do you think his reply was polite? Why?
Q: So how did she begin the conversation?

The teacher needs to consider when it is important to focus on questions of form and when to ignore the structure and focus on questions that will elicit responses that deal with the functional use of the language. For instance, some teachers spend more time with beginners and elementary learners helping them listen to the forms of the language, whereas more time will be given to listening to the functional uses of the language with higher level learners.

Task 6
Look at any activities from a listening textbook. Decide whether the questions that accompany the activities focus on form or function.

10.3.6 Visual Supported Questions Versus Nonvisual Supported Questions

Giving the learners some visual support while they listen to a spoken text enables them to comprehend the text better and answer questions more easily.

Visual support can mean watching the speaker talk (watching a video instead of listening to an audio recording) or looking at some textual support, such as a diagram or chart. For instance, while watching a video, the learner can pick up textual clues to help in forming answers to the teacher's questions. The learner then may be able to participate in the feedback session more than if only an audio cue were present. While using a textual support, the teacher can check comprehension by nonverbal means:

Q: Look at the map. Where was the man when he lost his wallet?

The learner can respond by pointing to the location on the map and hence demonstrate comprehension.

If the learner is encouraged to answer questions without reference to any graphic or textual material, the situation is more cognitively demanding than one in which the learner has some visual support. In this context, the types of questions the teacher asks should allow for loss of memory, or the learners' inability to express themselves clearly in the L2 (see earlier discussion). Initially, short display questions or Yes/No answers may be preferred.

Task 7
Examine a selection of listening activities from any general textbook. Look at the supporting visuals (if any). How do the visuals support comprehension? If there are no visuals to support a listening activity, prepare some (e.g., simple drawings on the board will help).

10.3.7 Individual Versus Group

Often when we think of asking questions in class, it is the teacher who asks and one student who responds. This type of individual work is important and very often is used effectively at the beginning of lessons to get things started. However, the type and number of questions asked can be changed if the learners work together to find the answers. Allowing learners to work in groups increases interaction and may increase the types of responses they make. If the teacher sets up listening tasks in which the learners' attention is focused on certain aspects of the text, and then they work together in a group to discover the answers, several things happen:

1. The focus is completely taken off testing comprehension and is placed on checking and evaluating listening.
2. Learners who initially have an incorrect answer may find out why they were wrong. In open class question/answer sessions, the teacher rarely

asks every student what he or she thinks the answer is to a question or allows discussion of why some answers are correct and others are not.

3. The teacher can set a variety of questions at different levels of difficulty. Then those students who can answer more challenging questions will help the members of their groups get the correct answers.

4. Learner cooperation is enhanced, and the focus is not on the teacher as role model for providing corrections to questions. Instead, classmates help each other.

5. Groups can be encouraged to go beyond the questions provided by the teacher and develop their own questions to answer in their groups. This may lead to the development of better listening strategies.

Task 8

Look at an extensive listening activity from a general textbook. With a partner, prepare a series of questions that encourage students to cooperate in finding the answers. Also consider the instructions you will give to the students to get them started on the task.

10.4 Questions and the Pedagogical Model

In this section, we suggest what we consider the most suitable types of questions for each of the eight dimensions in our model of listening (Chapter 6). Table 10.3 gives a summary of the dimensions and question types. It should be noted, though, that nearly any type of question can be asked for any of the dimensions – this is where the skill of the teacher comes in. The ticks in Table 10.3 suggest the types of questions that most easily lend themselves to developing listening in these dimensions. We have shaded in the other boxes to illustrate that it *might* be more difficult to use this type of question.

There are a few points to note in Table 10.3. First, the L1 and L2 can be used in any context to ask any type of question. This will depend on the level of the learners, the context in which the question is asked, and even the school policy on which language can be used in class. Second, an individual or a group can be asked questions from all eight dimensions. Here it may be a matter of either the teacher's personal preference or group dynamics – some students like working together whereas others do not. Third, all types of questions are suitable with the individual and strategic dimensions. In

Table 10.3 *The Most Productive Types of Questions to Use with the Dimensions of the Pedagogical Model*

	Display	Referential	Intensive	Extensive	L1	L2	Form	Function	Visual	Nonvisual	Individual	Group
Individualization	✓		✓		✓	✓	✓		✓	✓	✓	✓
Cross-cultural aspects		✓	✓	✓	✓	✓		✓			✓	✓
Social features					✓	✓	✓				✓	✓
Contextualized dimensions		✓		✓	✓	✓		✓	✓		✓	✓
Affective factors	✓	✓	✓	✓	✓	✓		✓	✓		✓	✓
Strategic aspects		✓		✓	✓	✓	✓	✓	✓		✓	✓
Intertextuality		✓			✓	✓				✓		✓
Critical discourse features		✓		✓	✓	✓	✓				✓	✓

these dimensions, the learners have more control over the type of listening they employ to gain comprehension, and consequently, the teacher should expose the learners to as wide a range of question types as possible in order to encourage them to develop different listening skills.

Our table is really only intended to illustrate the most productive types of questions that can be used with each dimension. For instance, referential and extensive questions lend themselves more to helping learners develop critical, cross-cultural, and intertextual dimensions than display or intensive questions do. In the cross-cultural dimension, if, after listening to an oral text on good writing habits, we ask a learner a Yes/No question such as

Q: Is plagiarism bad?
A: Yes.

we do not know whether the learner is simply making a guess at the answer or actually understands what plagiarism is. A better demonstration of comprehension would be to ask a referential question:

Q: Why is plagiarism bad?

On the other hand, when we consider the strategic dimension, answering a display question may be appropriate as a way for learners to illustrate that they used a strategy.

10.5 Conclusion

In this chapter, we have briefly examined the use of questions in developing listening skills. Using questions to develop comprehension should be seen as different from using questions to test listening. There are many types of questions that teachers can use, and each type of question helps learners develop more extensive listening skills. The types of questions need to be chosen to suit the listening dimensions being developed, and we suggest using different types of questions within the framework of the pedagogical model.

10.6 Discussion

1. We state that teaching and testing listening are separate issues. Explain why you agree or disagree.
2. Look at the two models for developing listening presented in Section 10.2. Discuss with a partner any variations you can make to these models.

3. Look at Table 10.2. Add to the list of advantages and disadvantages associated with focused and open questions.

4. For a monolingual context you are familiar with, what is the official policy of using the L1 in the classroom? Where does the policy originate? Why do you agree or disagree with the policy?

5. How important is visual support to the development of listening skills? Can we effectively develop listening skills without visual support? Why or why not?

6. Look at Table 10.3. Why would the dimensions represented by the shaded areas be more difficult to develop listening questions for?

11 Testing Listening

11.1 Introduction

In this last chapter, we present some of the main ways in which listening can be tested. Many of the types of questions associated with testing also appear in the teaching of listening (see Chapter 10). However, there are significant differences, or at least there should be, in how we ask questions to elicit comprehension and how similar types of questions are asked to test comprehension. This chapter on testing listening is necessarily brief; more complete discussions can be found in Brindley (1998), Buck (2001), Heaton (1990), Oller (1979), and Thomson (1995).

Buck (2001) tells us that there have been three historical developments in testing listening. These developments correspond to the theories of language learning and the different methods used to teach English over the past 60 years or so (see Chapter 1). These are the three approaches (see Table 11.1):

- the discrete-point approach
- the integrative approach
- the communicative approach

The discrete-point approach is derived from structuralism and behaviorism. The focus here is on the identification of isolated items of the language. That is, separate parts of the language are tested independently of each other; for instance, segmental phonemes, grammatical structures, and lexis are all treated as separate entities. The types of tests that can be used with the discrete-point approach are phonemic discrimination (identifying differences between phonemes), paraphrase recognition (reformulating what was heard), and response evaluation (responding appropriately to what was heard). The assumptions behind this type of approach to testing listening are that spoken text is the same as written text and that individual parts of the language can be isolated and tested. This is clearly not what listening is about, which the eight dimensions of our pedagogical model demonstrate.

Table 11.1 *Listening Test Types*

The Discrete-Point Approach		
Test Type	**Test Description**	**Example**
Phonemic discrimination tasks	Minimal pairs: Learners hear two words in which one phoneme is different. They must identify the difference in phonemes.	Choose the words with the /p/ sound in them: 1 2 pen Ben ball Paul bat Pat
Paraphrase recognition	Multiple choice: A context is given in this type of task. Listeners must reformulate what they hear.	Learners hear: *Mary asked her mother for some money to go to the cinema.* They read and choose one from: (a) Mary wanted money to buy some new clothes. (b) Mary wanted to see a movie so she asked for some money. (c) Mary asked her mother to go with her to the cinema.
Response evaluation	Multiple choice: Learners try to respond to what they hear.	Learners hear: *Would you like to go shopping?* They read and choose from: (a) Yes, okay. (b) Yes, I have. (c) It cost $200.

The Integrative Approach	
Test Type	**Test Description**
Gap-filling exercises	These types of tests assume that learners are able to fill in missing parts of language based on what they already know about the language. This is seen as reduced redundancy, that is, the ability to make predictions as a measure of language proficiency. Gap-fill (also known as cloze) exercises are more commonly associated with reading tests; however, a number of material designers and teachers also use this technique to test listening. First an oral text is selected. Then the tester goes through the text, removing certain words (often content words) or randomly removing every fifth, seventh, or ninth word from the taped text. Learners then hear the text and write down the missing words. This can be done with or without reference to the oral text in its written form (with blanks where the missing words are).
Dictation	It is claimed that dictation tests more than simple word recognition and spelling (see Oakerhott-Taylor 1977). It is seen as a synthesis of the speech perception process at the phonological, syntactic, and semantic levels and as such is an integrative testing technique.

Table 11.1 *(continued)*

The Integrative Approach *(continued)*	
Test Type	**Test Description**
Dictation (continued)	The technique is simple. The learners listen to an oral text and write down what they hear. The passage may be presented more than once, and it needs to be presented in segments, or information units, so the learner has time to process the language and write it down.
Sentence repetition activities	This is a variation on dictation tests. In this case, though, learners are not required to write down what they hear but to retell what they hear. Often the tester will record the responses and mark them later. This type of test is useful for nonliterate learners or young learners whose writing skills may not be well developed.
Statement evaluation	Learners evaluate the truth of a sentence. For instance, the learners hear: *When you go to the beach on a hot day you should drink plenty of water.* They then agree or disagree with the statement. Or they compare two sentences they hear and indicate whether the second sentence is true or not. (i) *The bus was very late.* (ii) *I took the bus and arrived at work on time.*
Translation	This may be seen as another version of a dictation test. However, in translation the learner needs to listen to the text in the L2 and write what is said in the L1. With translations there may be more than one correct way of expressing the concepts, so a system of being able to identify main information units is suggested. Furthermore, the tester needs to be bilingual to score such tests.

The Communicative Approach	
Features of Communicative Tests	**Description**
Authenticity	The most prominent feature of communicative tests is that the text that learners are required to listen to and the tasks that they need to perform, in response to the message, must have some relation to real-world use. Authenticity means different things to different people. However, the test text needs to be taken from authentic sources or contain features of real-life speech to be considered authentic. Buck (2001:86) gives a good example of this: Students are given a blank form to fill in with information about tourist events in London for a day. They listen to a text in which someone from the Tourist Information Office gives information about the types of day tours available and the listener fills in the information required to complete the form.

Table 11.1 *(continued)*

The Communicative Approach *(continued)*	
Features of Communicative Tests	**Description**
Authenticity *(continued)*	Although the text is not completely authentic, it does contain many features of spoken language (see Chapters 2 and 3). The task required of the listener, jotting down notes about the tours, may also be considered somewhat authentic.
Purposeful listening	Another feature of a communicative test is that there should seem to be a real purpose to the listening. For example, prior to listening to the test text, learners may be told that they are going to arrange a day out with their classmates and that they need to decide whether to aim for an indoor activity or an outdoor one. By listening to the weather forecast, they can then choose which activities are more suitable for that day. The listeners then listen to the weather forecast and choose from a list those activities that they might do in the morning, afternoon, and evening.

The information used in this table is explained in more detail in Buck 2001.

The integrative approach attempted to move away from the discrete measuring of language items by testing more than one item of language at a time. The main difference between the discrete-point approach to testing and the integrative approach is that in the former, the product is the focus of the assessment, whereas in the latter, the process becomes important. The techniques used with this approach are mainly gap-filling exercises, dictation, sentence repetition activities, statement evaluation, and translation (see Table 11.1). With the integrated approach, listeners must process spoken text and demonstrate that they understand the literal meaning of what is said. The main criticism here is that this type of test does not move much above the sentence level. Language is rarely tested in a wider context.

The communicative approach to testing attempts to account for listening and understanding in a wide range of contexts. It takes as its main orientation a demonstration by the listeners that they are able to do something with the information they have comprehended, that is, apply it to a wider communicative context. Language proficiency is seen as being able to demonstrate a degree of communicative competence (Hymes 1972). The characteristics of the communicative approach to testing follow (Weir 1990):

- The focus is on communicative performance as opposed to linguistic accuracy.
- Tests replicate as closely as possible conditions of actual performance.

- It is necessary to identify skills and performance conditions of language use in specific contexts.
- The sampling of relevant activities is important.
- The authenticity of task and genuineness of texts is important.
- Unsimplified language is used.
- A range of tests according to communicative purposes is needed.
- Tests will closely resemble communicative teaching activities, except that there will be no peer or teacher help.

Although the communicative approach is used extensively in teaching and testing, there are some problems with it. There is an enormous number of communicative events, and it is impossible to test them all. In addition, there are many ways to react to a situation, many more than it is possible to test. Being able to perform in one test situation does not necessarily mean that the testee will be able to perform well in other communicative situations. Furthermore, communicative tests are more difficult to prepare compared with discrete-point or integrative tests. However, communicative tests have had a significant influence on language testing in the past 30 years or so, and the basis of this type of testing probably fits our pedagogical model best. Two of the most important features of communicative tests that relate to the model, authenticity (e.g., social) and purposeful (e.g., contextual) listening, are illustrated in more detail in Table 11.1.

Understanding the approaches used in testing helps to frame our ideas about what and how to test. In this short chapter, it is difficult to give a full account on all the possible ins and outs of listening tests. However, it is important to consider what to test, how to test, and what to measure in any listening test.

Task 1

Use the information in Table 11.1 and examine a listening task in a general textbook. If you wanted to use this task for testing purposes, which type of test would you consider most suitable? What would you aim to test? Why?

11.2 What to Test

The type of listening test used will very much depend on the overall type of tests being administered. In *proficiency* and *placement* tests, the focus is on trying to discover what the learners know about the language. This is often done to determine which students to admit to specific courses. Therefore, the test designer will prepare general listening-type test items. A number of different test items are required for the learner to demonstrate overall listening abilities. There should also be degrees of difficulty in the test items, as the characteristics of such tests are to determine where the learner is in terms of proficiency level with respect to other learners; in other words, it is *norm-referenced*.

With *achievement* and *diagnostic* tests, the test designer has a different job. An achievement test aims to measure what the learners know after a course of instruction (i.e., how much learning has been achieved). A diagnostic test acts more like a needs analysis. The learners demonstrate what they can already do, and then the course designer develops material to raise their proficiency to the next level. Both achievement and diagnostic tests are *criterion-referenced*. A criterion-referenced test means that learners are assessed on a preagreed standard. They must reach a certain level of standard in order to pass the test. The learner's test score is interpreted with respect to the set criteria and is not measured against the scores of other students.

Once the type of test has been decided upon, the test designer can begin to prepare test items. These may be similar to the types of questions discussed in Chapter 10, so we shall not repeat them here. One point to note, however, is that achievement and diagnostic tests usually take place within existing language programs. Therefore, the teacher should use types of test questions that the learners have been exposed to during the course. It would not be appropriate to use certain types of questions in the teaching of a course and then use completely different types of questions in the tests – basically, the learners would then be tested on their ability to handle unknown testing procedures.

Task 2
Refer to the question types in Chapter 10. Try to identify the most suitable types of questions for proficiency, placement, achievement, and diagnostic tests.

11.3 How to Test

How a listening test is administered often depends on what the teaching environment is like. In privileged educational environments, the teacher most probably will have access to language laboratories or high-quality sound systems. In addition to this, the classrooms will be comfortable, with little or no outside noise to disturb the learners. On the other hand, many secondary school contexts, especially in developing countries, have little or no technology available, and the physical conditions under which the learners take tests may be challenging. Such schools need to marshal whatever technical support is available and take steps to reduce the possibility of external factors affecting the learners' performance on tests. Before preparing listening tests, some of the following questions need to be considered:

- What approach to testing will be taken?
- What type of test is being developed (proficiency, placement, achievement, diagnostic)?
- What technology is available or required?
- What will happen in case of technical problems? Is there a backup plan?
- Where will the texts come from? Will they be commercial, adapted, or teacher-produced texts?
- Will the learners have access to visual support as well as the audio message? How will this affect comprehension?
- Will the learners be presented with authentic texts or not?
- Will the learners listen to texts spoken by native or nonnative English speakers?
- By means of what type of test items will learners demonstrate their comprehension?
- Who will take the test?
- How many learners will take the test?
- Will the learners take the test as a whole group listening together, or in a language lab with earphones?
- Who will supervise the test?
- What are the test conditions likely to be?
- Can physical factors that might affect performance be eliminated (e.g., closing windows, turning off noisy air conditioners)?
- How will the test be collected?
- How will the test be marked?

Task 3

Think about a listening test you can prepare for a specified group of learners you are familiar with. How many of the preceding questions can you answer? Are some easier to answer than others? Why?

Table 11.2 *A Selection of Tests and the Skills They Test*

Description of Test	Skills Tested
Learners listen to a description while they look at several pictures. They choose the picture that is being described.	Listening
The learner has a conversation with an examiner or with other testees. The student's ability to interact and respond appropriately to the dialogue is measured.	Listening and speaking
Learners listen to a dialogue and then choose the best answers from multiple-choice statements.	Listening and reading
Learners listen to a story and then write a summary of the story.	Listening and writing
Learners listen to an oral text. They read questions about the text. Then they write full sentence answers to the questions.	Listening, reading, and writing

11.4 What to Measure

In developing listening tests, the preceding checklist of questions may prove useful. However, the test designer needs to consider seriously whether it is only listening that the test measures. In many instances, the learners are also tested on other skills. If students happen to be weak in, say, reading, this may adversely affect their ability to demonstrate their listening skills. Table 11.2 lists some common types of tests that are used to measure "listening" but that actually involve language skills too.

As can be seen from Table 11.2, it is very easy for the tester to think that the only skill being tested is listening. However, the learner's ability to handle other language skills is also important and the success or failure of the learner on the test may rest not so much with their listening ability but with their reading, writing, or speaking proficiencies.

Thompson (1995: 4–5) outlines some factors to consider when preparing listening tests:

- The closer the text is to oral rather than written text, the more appropriate it is for testing listening.
- Visual support is particularly helpful for lower proficiency learners.
- Test passages should be short, around two or three minutes.
- Consideration should be given to the amount of prior knowledge that learners may require to comprehend the text.
- Specialized vocabulary needs to be avoided in general listening tests.
- Simplifying oral texts does not necessarily help the learner.

Table 11.3 *Types of Test Validity*

Type of Validity	Description
Face validity	This refers to whether a listening test looks like a listening test. If a test looks like it has been designed to test listening skills, then it has face validity. The easiest way to determine validity is to ask colleagues to look at a test and tell you what it is measuring. Their answers will either confirm or nullify the face validity of the test.
Content validity	This refers to the degree to which the test actually measures the language it is intended to measure. With achievement and diagnostic tests, the test items must be in the course content. With placement and proficiency tests, the content should try to measure different facets of listening (e.g., if a test had a lot of phonemic discrimination but no items on stress and intonation, it probably would not have high content validity).
Construct validity	This refers to the relationship of the test to the approaches of language learning in a course. For instance, if a course approach is based on behaviorism, then a communicative listening test would not have construct validity.

Empirical validity	Empirical validity is the relationship of the test results to some other form of measurement, such as
	   – other valid test scores,
	   – teachers' ratings,
	   – later performance on other tests.
	In this way, if test scores match some other criteria for measurement, the test is considered empirically valid.

- Inserting macro-markers may aid comprehension (e.g., Today I am going to talk about . . .).
- Speech rates that are very fast (above 200 wpm) should be avoided.

In any discussion about what is being measured in language testing, we come across the words *validity* and *reliability* (see Heaton 1990 for a full account of these terms and of preparing tests). Test validity refers to whether the test appears to test what it is intended to test. If, for example, we ask learners in West Africa to listen to a description of a Hawaiian wedding, and the learner does not even know where Hawaii is, then we are testing more than simple comprehension: We are testing world knowledge, the ability to deal with a lot of new vocabulary, and unfamiliar concepts. Table 11.3 illustrates the different types of validity we have to consider in test construction.

Reliability refers to the consistency of the test. In other words, if two different markers mark the test, will they get the same scores? Or, if the same marker marks the test on two different occasions, will the result be the same? Or, if the testee takes the exam twice, will the scores be the same? Some of the factors that can affect test reliability follow:

- *The number of test items.* Is there a big enough range of test items in the test to measure listening skills, or is the test a measure of only one aspect of listening?
- *The administration of the test.* Is the test administered in the same way each time it is given?
- *Test instructions.* Are the instructions clear so that all testees can follow them?
- *Personal/environmental factors.* Are the conditions for taking the test appropriate? For example, no one is sick, and the room is adequate for the purpose of a test.
- *Scoring.* What kind of scoring techniques are used? Objective tests – tests that have agreed-upon answers – usually have higher reliability levels than subjectively marked tests – tests in which individual markers decide on the correctness of the answer.

Task 4

Look at the following ESP listening test, prepared for first-year university engineering students. Is the test measuring listening only, or does it also require the testee to use other language/knowledge skills? Do you consider the test to be valid and reliable?

Notes to Teacher: The video is 11 minutes 40 seconds long. Show the complete video twice. Follow this time frame:

First viewing (11 minutes 40 seconds)

Break for students to organize their notes (5 minutes)

Second viewing (11 minutes 40 seconds)

Complete notes (10 minutes)

Summary writing (30 minutes)

Listening Test

1. Watch the video and complete the following skeleton notes.
   MANUFACTURING PROCESSES
   Primary process =
   Secondary process =
      a. Casting and moulding =
      b. Forming =
      c. Separating =
      d. Conditioning =
      e. Assembly =
      f. Finishing =

2. Use the notes that you have made from the video to write a 100-word summary of the manufacturing process.

11.5 How to Assess Listening

There are many ways to mark tests: percentage points, number scales, grade points, descriptors, and performance criteria. Whereas the discrete-point and the integrative approaches favor more detailed marking by numbers or grades, the communicative approach tends toward more holistic marking, such as descriptors (also known as performance indicators or task criteria). Figure 11.1 shows some scales that might be used to assess listening.

The complexity of the pedagogical model presented in Chapter 6 may pose a challenge to the tester. As there are eight dimensions to the model, the test designer first needs to consider which of the dimensions are inherent in the listening activity and which could, or should, be tested. As we have stated elsewhere in this book, it may be impossible to account for all dimensions of the model in each listening situation. Therefore, the test designer needs to use the evaluation checklist (Table 6.1) to assess the degree to which each dimension is represented in the activity. On the basis of this evaluation, the tester can decide on the type of tests that are appropriate. After designing the tests, one of the scoring measures suggested in Table 11.1 may be used, or the tester might consider developing more complete descriptors.

Examples of descriptors for listening can be found in Carroll and West (1989). These authors provide details of how to construct test descriptors,

Percentage Scale	Number Scale	Grade Points	Limited Description Scale
0	0	F	Nonscorable
10	1	E	Limited
20			
30			
40	2	D	Adequate
50			
60	3	C	Good
70			
80	4	B	Very Good
90			
100	5	A	Excellent

Figure 11.1 Scales used for measuring listening

which they refer to as yardsticks. They use nine-point scales, with descriptions, of what listeners should be able to do at each level. For example, at point 9 the listeners should be able to handle "all general listening operations, as well as those in own specialist areas, with confidence and competence similar to those in own mother tongue" and extract "the full content of the message without undue need for repetition or repair," among other things. At level 5 the listener is expected only to handle "moderate-level listening operations with competence and confidence" and to extract "major points of message but with frequent loss of detail and subtlety." At level 1 a listener can handle "only the simplest listening operations such as short isolated exchanges (e.g., greetings, giving times, prices) and with little confidence" and extract "only basic or predicted messages, or those translated using a dictionary or phrase book."

Task 5
Choose one of the dimensions from the pedagogical model presented in Chapter 6 and write test descriptors for the dimensions. Limit the number of descriptors to five levels.

11.6 Conclusion

This final chapter has highlighted some of the important issues related to testing listening comprehension. Developing valid and reliable listening language tests is a complex process. This is because the processes of listening are hidden from the tester, and so the ways to measure the ability to handle spoken text are more demanding. Three main approaches have been used to test listening, and there are many ways in which listening tests can be devised. We maintain that the communicative approach offers the most opportunity for learners to demonstrate their comprehension ability, and we propose that this approach can be used in a flexible way with the pedagogical model presented in Chapter 6 for listening.

11.7 Discussion

1. Which of the three approaches to testing listening are you most familiar with? Which one do you prefer using as a learner or teacher? Why?

2. Look at Table 11.1. Can you think of any other test types?

3. Do you think that it is correct to try to isolate listening to measure it by itself, or should we integrate listening with other skills? Why or why not?

4. Which of the types of test validity (Table 11.3) do you consider the most important? Why?

5. We argue for a flexible approach toward testing listening, so that learners can be tested on different listening abilities based on the pedagogical model presented in Chapter 6. Explain why you agree or disagree. How easy or difficult is it to test different listening abilities with the new model?

Appendix
Concluding Questions for Reflection

In this section, we suggest a list of essay and project titles and topics. The reader may wish to consider these as "tests" of their knowledge on teaching and developing listening skills. If this book has been used as a core text, the instructor may consider setting some of the essays or projects as part of the course assessment.

Essays

Write a 3,000-word essay on one of the following topics:

1. Explain how different approaches to language learning have affected the ways in which listening has been taught in the classroom. Give your views on the effectiveness of each method.
2. How do the various features of speech affect how we teach listening?
3. How do language objectives and learning objectives differ? Illustrate how they can be combined in a listening task.
4. Critique the eight dimensions for listening (Chapter 6) and show, with examples, how they can be incorporated into a listening task.
5. Discuss the effectiveness of technology in the classroom as an aid to teaching listening.

Projects and Presentations

Prepare and present a project on listening based on one of the following ideas:

1. Choose a general textbook and critically examine a selection of listening tasks in the book. Select at least two tasks each from the beginning, middle, and end of the book. Prepare additional exercises to accompany the tasks so as to enhance learners' listening skills.
2. Use the guideline questions about the dimensions of listening in Chapter 6 to prepare five listening activities for a group of learners of your choice.

3. Select some authentic listening material. Prepare exercises to accompany the material. Explain the rationale behind the selection of the material and the approach taken in preparing the activities.
4. Design a specific listening course for a group of learners at the elementary language level. The situation is as follows: large class (40+), low motivation, poor educational environment, only technology is a tape recorder.
5. Design a specific listening course for a group of intermediate level learners. The situation is as follows: small group (20), high motivation, good educational environment, and sophisticated technological support.

In preparing your projects, consider

- age of learners
- language level
- approaches to learning and syllabus type
- general aims and objectives
- specific aims and objectives
- dimensions to listening
- technology to be used
- type of questioning and feedback to learners
- evaluation of the materials

References

Abbs, B., and Freebairn, I. 1993. *Blueprint. Upper intermediate.* Harlow: Longman.

Baltova, I. 1994. The impact of video on the comprehension skills of core French students. *The Canadian Modern Language Review.* 50 3: 507–31.

Bartlett, F. C. 1932. *Remembering.* Cambridge: Cambridge University Press.

Beglar, D., and Murray, N. 1993. *Contemporary topics: Advanced listening comprehension.* White Plains: Longman.

Biggs, J. B. 1987. *Student approaches to learning and studying.* Hawthorn, Victoria: Australian Council for Educational Research.

Blundell, L., and Stokes, J. 1981. *Task Listening.* Cambridge: Cambridge University Press.

Bourne, L. E., Dominowski, R. L., and Loftus, E. F. 1979. *Cognitive processes.* Englewood Cliffs, NJ: Prentice Hall.

Bowler, B., and Cunningham, S. 1991. *Headway pronunciation: Upper-intermediate.* Oxford: Oxford University Press.

Brennam, M., and Woodbury Miller, J. 1982. Making an English language teaching videotape. *ELT Journal* 36, 3: 169–74.

Brett, P. 1997. A comparative study of the effects of the use of multimedia on listening comprehension. *System* 25, 1: 39–53.

Brindley, G. 1998. Assessing listening abilities. *Annual Review of Applied Linguistics* 18: 171–91.

Brown, A. L., and Palincsar, A. S. 1982. Inducing strategic learning from texts by means of informed, self-control training. *Topics in Learning and Learning Disabilities* 2, 1: 1–17.

Brown, G. 1987. Twenty-five years of teaching listening comprehension. *English Teaching Forum* 25, 4: 11–15.

Brown, G. 1990. *Listening to spoken English.* Harlow: Longman.

Brown, G., and Yule, G. 1983. *Teaching the spoken language: An approach based on the analysis of conversational English.* Cambridge: Cambridge University Press.

Buck, G. 2001. *Assessing listening*. Cambridge: Cambridge University Press.

Caroll, J. B., and West, R. 1989. *ESU framework: Performance scales for English language testing*. Harlow: Longman.

Chen, H. 1999. Guidelines for evaluating ESL listening resources on the World Wide Web. In B. Morrison, D. Cruikshank, D. Gardner, J. James, and K. Keobke (eds.), *Information Technology and Multimedia in English Language Teaching*. Hong Kong: Hong Kong English Language Centre: The Hong Kong Polytechnic Univeristy. pp. 185–204.

Clark, H. H. 1996. *Using language*. New York: Cambridge University Press.

Crombie, W. 1985a. *Discourse and language learning: A relational approach to syllabus design*. Oxford: Oxford University Press.

Crombie, W. 1985b. *Process and relation in discourse and language learning*. Oxford: Oxford University Press.

Cunningham, S., and Bowler, B. 1990. *Headway: Intermediate pronunciation*. Oxford: Oxford University Press.

De Casper, A. J., and Fifer, W. P. 1980. Of human bondage: Newborns prefer their mothers' voices. *Science* 208: 1174–6.

De Casper, A. J., and Spence, M. 1986. Prenatal maternal speech influences newborns' perceptions of speech sounds. *Infant Behaviour and Infant Development* 9: 133–50.

Derry, S. J., and Murphy, D. A. 1986. Designing systems that train learning ability: From theory to practice. *Review of Educational Research* 56: 1–39.

Disick, R. S. 1975. *Individualization of instruction: Strategies and methods*. New York: Harcourt Brace Jovanovich.

Eastman, D. 2001. Listening: Web sites for the language teacher. *ELT Journal* 55, 4: 420–2.

Ellis, G., and Sinclair, B. 1989. *Learning to learn English*. Cambridge: Cambridge University Press.

Fairclough, N. 1992. *Discourse and social change*. Cambridge: Polity Press.

Fairclough, N., and Wodak, R. 1997. Critical discourse analysis. In T. A. Van Dijk (ed.), *Discourse studies: A multidisciplinary introduction. Volume 2. Discourse as social interaction*. London: Sage. pp. 258–84.

Field, J. 1998. Skills and strategies: Towards a new methodology for listening. *ELT Journal* 52, 2: 110–18.

Flavell, J. H. 1979. Metacognitive and cognitive monitoring. *American Psychologist* 34, 10: 906–11.

Flowerdew, J., and Miller, L. 1992. Student perceptions, problems and strategies in L2 lectures. *RELC Journal* 23, 2: 60–80.

Flowerdew, J., and Miller, L. 1995. On the notion of culture in second language lectures. *TESOL Quarterly* 29, 2: 345–74.

Flowerdew, J., and Miller, L. 1996. Lectures in a second language: Notes towards a cultural grammar. *English for Specific Purposes* 15, 2: 345–73.

Gardner, D., and Miller, L. (eds.). 1996. *Tasks for independent language learning*. Alexandria: TESOL.

Gardner, D., and Miller, L. (eds.). 1997. *A study of tertiary level self-access facilities in Hong Kong*. Evaluation of the Student Experience Project, City University of Hong Kong. Hong Kong.

Gardner, D., and Miller, L. 1999. *Establishing self-access: From theory to practice*. Cambridge: Cambridge University Press.

Garis, E. 1997. Movies in the language classroom: Dealing with problematic content. *TESOL Journal* 6, 4: 20–3.

Goh, C. 1997. Metacognitive awareness and second language listeners. *ELT Journal* 41, 4: 361–9.

Graus, J. 1999. *An evaluation of the usefulness of the internet in the EFL classroom*. Unpublished MA Thesis. University of Nijmegen, The Netherlands. Available: *http://home.plex.nl/~jgraus*.

Grice, H. P. 1975. Logic and conversation. In P. Cole and J. L. Morgan (eds.), *Syntax and semantics 3: Speech acts*. New York: Academic Press. pp. 41–58.

Halliday, M. A. K. 1989. *Spoken and written language*. Oxford: Oxford University Press.

Halliday, M. A. K. 1994. *An introduction to functional grammar*. London: Edward Arnold.

Halliday, M. A. K., and Hasan, R. 1976. *Cohesion in English*. London: Longman.

Heaton, J. B. 1990. *Writing English language tests* (2nd ed.). London: Longman.

Henly, E. 1993. *Focus on American culture*. Englewood Cliff, NJ: Regents/Prentice Hall.

Hoey, M. P. 1983. *On the surface of discourse*. London: Allen and Unwin.

Holt, R. 1999. *On target!* Hong Kong: Oxford University Press.

Howatt, A. P. R. 1984. *A history of English language teaching*. Oxford: Oxford University Press.

Hymes, D. 1972. On communicative competence: Extracts. In J. B. Pride and J. Holmes (eds.), *Sociolinguistics*. Harmondsworth: Penguin. pp. 269–93.

Jones, L., and Kimbrough, V. 1997. *Great ideas*. New York: Cambridge University Press.

Kenelfield, G. 1977. Progress report of the schools television research project, Part II. *Eduational Television International* 3, 3.

Kumaravadivelu, B. 1991. Language-learning tasks: Teacher intention and learner interpretation. *ELT Journal* 45, 2: 98–107.

Kyriacou, C., Benmansoure, N., and Low, G. 1996. Pupil learning styles and foreign language learning. *Language Learning Journal* 13: 22–4.

Lado, R., and Fries, C. C. 1958. *English pronunciation: Exercises in sound segments intonation and rhythm*. Ann Arbor: University of Michigan Press.

Laleman, J. P., and Priess, R. 1994. *Manufacturing technology* [video recording]. Bloomington, IL: Meridian Education Corporation.

Lee, W. Y-C. 1995. Authenticity revisited: Text authenticity and learner authenticity. *ELT Journal* 49, 4: 323–8.

Littlewood, W. 1981. *Communicative language teaching: An introduction* Cambridge: Cambridge University Press.

Littlewood, W. 1996. Autonomy in communication and learning in the Asian context. In *Proceedings of Autonomy 2000: The development of learning independence in language learning*. King Mongkut's Institute of Technology, Thonburi, Bangkok. pp. 124–40.

Lonergan, J. 1984. *Video in language teaching*. Cambridge: Cambridge University Press.

Long, M. H., and Crookes, G. 1992. Three approaches to task-based syllabus design. *TESOL Quarterly* 26, 1: 27–56.

MacWilliam, I. 1986. Video and language comprehension. *ELT Journal* 40, 2: 131–5.

Mathewson, G. C. 1985. Toward a comprehensive model of affect in the reading process. In H. Singer and R. B. Ruddell (eds.), *Theoretical models and processes of reading* (3rd edition). New York, Delaware: International Reading Association. pp. 841–56.

Mendelsohn, D. J. 1994. Learning to listen: A strategy-based approach for the second language learner. San Diego: Dominie Press.

Miller, L. 2001. English for engineering. In J. Murphy and P. Byrd (eds.), *Understanding the courses we teach: Local perspectives on English language teaching*. Ann Arbor: University of Michigan Press.

Morley, J. 1995. Academic listening comprehension instruction: Models, principles, and practice. In D. Mendelsohn and J. Rubin (eds.), *A guide for the teaching of second language listening*. San Diego: Dominie Press.

Morrow, K. 1981. Principles of communicative methodology. In K. Johnson and K. Morrow (eds.), *Communication in the classroom: Application and methods for a communicative approach*. Harlow: Longman.

Nelson, J. 1997. *A system for the evaluation of ESL web sites.* Unpublished MA Thesis. College of Graduate Studies, University of Idaho. Available: *http://www.ialc.wsu.edu/eslint/thesisindex.html.*

Nunan, D. 1996. What's my style? In D. Gardner and L. Miller (eds.), *Tasks for independent language learning.* Alexandria: TESOL.

Nyikos, M. 1990. Sex-related differences in adult language learning: Socialization and memory factors. *The Modern Language Journal* 74, iii: 273–87.

Oakeshatt-Taylor, A. 1977. Dictation as a test of listening comprehension. In R. Dirven (ed.), *Listening comprehension in foreign language teaching.* Kronberg: Scriptor.

Ochs, E. 1979. Planned and unplanned discourse. In T. Givon (ed.), *Syntax and semantics. Vol. 12. Discourse and Syntax.* New York and London: Academic Press. pp. 51–80.

Oller, J. W., Jr. 1979. *Language tests at school.* London: Longman.

O'Malley, J. M., and Chamot, A. U. 1990. *Learning strategies in second language acquisition.* Cambridge: Cambridge University Press.

O'Malley, J. M., Chamot, A. U., and Kupper, L. 1989. Listening comprehension strategies in second language acquisition. *Applied Linguistics* 10, 4: 418–37.

O'Malley, J. M., Chamot, A. U., Stewner-Manzanares, G., Russo, R. P., and Kupper, L. 1985. Learning strategies applications with students of English as a second language. *TESOL Quarterly* 19, 3: 557–84.

Owens, R. E. 1996. *Language development* (4th ed.). Boston: Allyn and Bacon.

Oxford, R. L. 1989. Use of language learning strategies: A synthesis of studies with implications for strategy training. *System* 17, 2: 235–47.

Oxford, R. L. 1990. *Language learning strategies: What every teacher should know.* Boston: Heinle and Heinle.

Parsons, R. D., Lewis Hinson, S., and Sardo-Brown, D. 2001. *Educational psychology: A practitioner-researcher model of teaching.* Stamford: Wadsworth/Thomson.

Piaget, J. 1959. *The language and thought of the child.* New York: Harcourt Brace Jovanovich.

Radley, P., and Sharley, A. 1999. *Trio 2.* Oxford: Heinemann Education Books.

Reid, J. M. 1987. The learning style preferences of ESL students. *TESOL Quarterly* 21, 1: 87–111.

Richards, J. C. 1993. Beyond the text book: The role of commercial materials in language teaching. *RELC Journal* 24, 1: 1–14.

Richards, J. C., and Rogers, T. S. 2001. *Approaches and methods in language teaching: A description and analysis*. Cambridge: Cambridge University Press

Rixon, S. 1987. *Listening: Upper-intermediate*. Oxford: Oxford University Press.

Roberts, M. B. 1986. *Biology: A functional approach* (4th ed.). Edinburgh: Thomas Nelson.

Ross, R. N. 1975. Ellipsis and the structure of expectation. *San Jose State occasional papers in linguistics* 1: 183–91.

Rost, M. 1994. *Introducing listening*. London: Penguin English Applied Linguistics.

Rumelhart, D. E. 1975. Notes on a schema for stories. In D. G. Bobrow and A. Collins (eds.), *Representation and understanding: Studies in cognitive science*. New York: Academic Press.

Sacks, H., Schegloff, E. A., and Jefferson, G. 1974. A simplest systematics for the organization of turn-taking for conversation. *Language* 50, 4: 696–735.

Schank, R. C., and Abelson, R. 1977. *Scripts, plans, goals and understanding*. Hillsdale, NJ: Erlbaum.

Scollon, R., and Scollon. S. W. 2001. *Intercultural communication: A discourse approach* (2nd ed.). Malden, MA: Blackwell.

Shannon, C. E., and Weaver, W. 1949. *The mathematical theory of communication*. Urbana: University of Illinois Press.

Sperber, D., and Wilson, D. 1986. *Relevance: Communication and cognition*. Oxford: Blackwell.

Stern, H. H. 1983. *Fundamental concepts of language teaching*. Oxford: Oxford University Press.

Tannen, D. 1979. What's in a frame? Surface evidence for underlying expectations. In R. O. Freedle (ed.), *New directions in discourse processing*. Norwood, NJ: Ablex. pp. 137–81.

Thomas, J. 1995. *Meaning in interaction: An introduction to pragmatics*. London and New York: Longman.

Thompson, I. 1995. Assessment of second/foreign language listening comprehension. In D. J. Mendelsohn and J. Rubin (eds.), *A guide for the teaching of second language listening*. San Diego: Dominie Press.

Thompson, I. 2000. *Criteria for evaluating software*. Available: *http://www. nflrc.hawaii.edu//ithompson/flmedia/skill-frame-1.htm*.

Tomalin, B. 1986. *Video, TV & radio in the English class*. London: Macmillan.

Tsui, A. B. M., and Fullilove, J. 1998. Bottom-up or top-down processing as a discriminator of L2 listening performance. *Applied Linguistics* 19, 9: 432–51.

Tyacke, M., and Mendelsohn, D. 1986. Student needs: Cognitive as well as communicative. *TESL Canada Journal, Special Issue* 1: 171–83.

Ur, P. 1994. *Teaching listening comprehension.* Cambridge: Cambridge University Press.

Vandergrift, L. 1997. The comprehension strategies of second language (French) listeners: A descriptive study. *Foreign Language Annals* 30, 3: 387–409.

van Dijk, T. A. 1977. *Text and context: Explorations in the semantics and pragmatics of discourse.* London: Longman

van Dijk, T. A. 1997. Discourse as interaction in society. In T. A. van Dijk (ed.), *Discourse studies: A multidisciplinary introduction. Vol. 2. Discourse as Social Interaction.* London: Sage. pp. 1–37.

Violand-Sanchez, E. 1995. Cognitive and learning styles of high school students: Implications for ESL curriculum development. In J. M. Reid (ed.), *Learning styles in the ESL/EFL classroom.* Boston: Heinle and Heinle.

Warschauer, M., and Healey, D. 1998. Computers and language learning: An overview. *Language Teaching* 31: 57–71.

Weir, C. 1990. *Communicative language testing.* New York: Prentice Hall.

Weistein, C. E., and Mayer, R. E. 1986. The teaching of learning strategies. In M. C. Wittrock (ed.), *Handbook of research on teaching.* New York: Macmillan. pp. 315–27.

Wenden, A. 1991. *Learner strategies for learner autonomy.* Great Britain: Prentice Hall International.

Werker, J. F., and Tess, R. C. 1984. Cross-language speech perception: Evidence for perceptual reorganization during the first year of life. *Infant Behaviour and Development* 7: 49–63.

Willing, K. 1985. *Learning styles in adult migrant education.* National Curriculum Resource Centre for Adult Migrant Education Program: Adelaide.

Willing, K. 1988. Learning strategies as information management: Some definitions for a theory of learning strategies. *Prospect* 3, 2: 139–55.

Willing, K. 1989. *Teaching how to learn.* National Centre for English Language Teaching and Research: Sydney.

Witkin, H., Moore, C., Goodenough, D., and Cox, P. 1977. Field-dependent and field-independent cognitive styles and their educational implications. *Review of Educational Research* 47: 1–64.

Wong, M. C. P. 1996. Focus on your language needs. In D. Gardner and L. Miller (eds.), *Tasks for independent language learning.* Alexandria: TESOL.

Index